SECRETS FROM INSIDE THE
CLUBHOUSE

SECRETS FROM INSIDE THE CLUBHOUSE

What Men **REALLY** Think About Women

RON STOUT

BROWN BOOKS
PUBLISHING GROUP

Secrets from Inside the Clubhouse
What Men REALLY Think About Women

© 2009 Ron Stout

All rights reserved. No part of this publication may be used or reproduced in any manner whatsoever without written permission except in the case of brief quotations embodied in critical articles and reviews.

Manufactured in the United States of America.

For information, please contact:

Brown Books Publishing Group
16200 North Dallas Parkway, Suite 170
Dallas, Texas 75248
www.brownbooks.com
972-381-0009

A New Era in Publishing™

Hardbound ISBN-13: 978-1-934812-34-1
Hardbound ISBN-10: 1-934812-34-X

Paperback ISBN-13: 978-1-934812-35-8
Paperback ISBN-10: 1-934812-35-8

LCCN: 2009920417

www.clubhousebook.com

For Logan and Austin,
May yours always be a blooming of the sexes,
not a battle.

Contents

| Chapter 1: | Inquiring Minds Simply Must Know . . . . 1 |
| Chapter 2: | We *Had* Our Manhood When We Came in Here! . . .7 |

Sex

Chapter 3:	Electrical Plugs and Wall Sockets 25
Chapter 4:	Pocket Rockets and Performance Anxiety 31
Chapter 5:	Penis Recon. 37
Chapter 6:	Haste Makes Chaste. 47
Chapter 7:	It's Helga from Helsinki! 53

Work

Chapter 8:	Man the Torpedoes . . . the Patriarchy Is in Trouble!. . 59
Chapter 9:	The Honey-Do Paradigm Shift 67
Chapter 10:	June Cleaver Has a Briefcase? 73
Chapter 11:	The Worm Has Turned 77
Chapter 12:	Chivalry Is an Honor, Not an Order. 85

Money

Chapter 13:	Just Whose Money Is This Anyway? 91
Chapter 14:	Platinum Cards and White Tablecloths 97
Chapter 15:	Pocket Charm Works Both Ways 105

| Chapter 16: | Women Need to PEEPEE .... 109 |
| Chapter 17: | Firing Off Financial Pheromones .... 119 |

SPORTS AND SUPERHEROES

Chapter 18:	Female Pectoralis Major 125
Chapter 19:	Torn Tendons and Ripped Rotator Cuffs 131
Chapter 20:	Robbing Peter to Pay Paula 137
Chapter 21:	The Thrill of Victory and the Agony of Defeat .. 145
Chapter 22:	It's a Bird! It's a Plane! It's . . . a WOMAN! 153
Chapter 23:	Don't Quit Your Day Job 159
Chapter 24:	Donning Fatigues like the Traditional Man ... 167

HEAD OF HOUSEHOLD

Chapter 25:	Toilet Seats and Dirty Underwear 173
Chapter 26:	A *Woman's* Home Is Her Castle? 179
Chapter 27:	¿Cómo Se Dice la Jefa en Inglés? 189

FEMININE PRIVILEGE

| Chapter 28: | Yesterday All Our Troubles Seemed So Far Away .. 197 |

IT'S A REAL, REAL, REAL, REAL WORLD

| Chapter 29: | Have Women Become the Superior Sex? ......207 |
| Chapter 30: | The Ultimate Secret .... 215 |

Acknowledgments

You've no doubt heard the phrase, "It takes a village to raise a child." Writing this book, at least for me, involved a similar dynamic. Although I wrote the words in relative solitude, the end result of my work became a product I could not have accomplished alone. Many people helped raise me as I grew from a neonate scribe to a published author.

First, to my sons, Logan and Austin, and my daughters-in-law, Haley and Anneliz, I extend my warmest thanks. Their love and support helped see this project through to completion. I am so blessed to be able to share my life and love with them.

Special thanks go to my good friend Deborah Causwell. She was my muse from beginning to end and was always willing to take the time to listen and provide constructive critiques of my many, and sometimes incongruent, ideas. Her help was immeasurable. Thanks also go to Tom Leach, Will Robertson, Elaine McDade, and Sandy Stout for enduring my many readings and requests for feedback as I completed the manuscript. Their input and support is greatly appreciated. And a special thank-you to Sandy for pushing me to "Turn it in, or it will never go anywhere!" I also want to thank Dr. Gary John and the members of his men's group who provided valuable input and analysis. Thanks go to Andrea Goldreich for introducing me to Cindy Birne of Brown Books Publishing Group and to Gloria Tostado and Chris Hann for hosting a roundtable discussion group whose arguments and feedback early on helped me better shape my content.

To the fine folks at Brown Books, thanks go to Milli Brown for encouraging me to take a chance on a controversial book and for putting together such a first-class organization. From start to finish, everyone at Brown treated me with respect and supported me in my efforts. Thanks to Kathryn Grant for her steady guidance as she oversaw the process from idea to publication. Special thanks go to Joy Tipping for her content editing. She played a critical "first responder" role as she helped me shape the content and temper the tone. To Bill Young for his on-the-mark illustrations, cover design, and artistic creativity. What it took me thousands of words to convey, he did both humorously and succinctly in seven creative illustrations. I'd also like to thank Jessie Stephens for her quality line editing and Cindy Birne for bringing me in to the Brown family.

My most grateful and special thanks go to my chief editor, Dr. Janet Harris. Her wisdom and incredible insight helped me more than words can describe. Her vision and valuable input helped shape my content and convinced me to share the "secrets" men think but don't tell women. She tossed me a ring buoy when I needed it most in the high seas of composition and effectively saved me from myself. This book would simply not be the same without her.

I'd also like to thank all of the women and men who participated in the many focus groups I facilitated throughout the country. Each and every one of them was of great assistance to me as I conducted my research. Finally, I'd like to thank all of the men who shared their stories, their thoughts, and their feelings about how life has changed for men in America. This book is about them and voices their message to women and men everywhere.

1

INQUIRING MINDS SIMPLY MUST KNOW

What would happen if women were no longer around to tell men what to do? What would happen if men were no longer around to do what they were told? Would women meander about trying to find somebody to manage while men meandered about trying to find someone *not* to listen to? And would they miss each other? Women might miss men more than they'd be missed by men. Men would be fine as long as they had a beer, a newspaper, some toenail clippers, and the remote control. But women might not fare too well in a world sans men, with no one around to supervise. And if a man said something in the forest and a woman wasn't there to hear him, would he still be wrong?

Men actually think about this stuff; they just don't tell women. They think about a lot of stuff, especially men over forty since they have experienced firsthand the wholly transformed cultural roles of women in America. In fact, there's an unwritten but well-understood code among men when sharing what they really think about how women have changed. Every guy knows about it. It's a fraternal affiliation, a support group of sorts, a virtual clubhouse where no one is allowed inside without a penis and a pair of testicles. It's the one place where guys can unload the secrets they think about but would never tell the girls.

Women have never been able to make it past the bouncer at this very private and coveted clubhouse—until now. For the first time, they have the opportunity to sneak in the back door and hear what men are saying. This book is their ticket inside the hallowed halls of the "boys club." *Secrets from Inside the Clubhouse* is the first book of its kind to share the long-overdue *male* perspective on how women's roles have changed. It is also the key that unlocks the vault of secrets men think about but don't say, the very secrets women everywhere want to know.

The More Things Change . . .

To uncover the secrets men think but don't say, you'll hear from over one hundred guys, among more than five hundred interviewed, willing to be featured in the book. One is even a member of the Temporary Abstinence Movement (TAM). All these men candidly share how they feel about hyperaggressive women in the bedroom, having women as bosses, and having wives or girlfriends who make more money than they do. And they're especially in a quandary about whether it's still acceptable to open a door for a woman, who should pay the check at dinner, and whether a casual, platonic hug will be misinterpreted and labeled sexual harassment. They're even confused about how to shake hands!

A lot of the men said that these days they feel under attack, blamed for everything bad that has ever happened to women. Some added they feel guilty for being born male. Others said that at times they even feel like women want them to apologize just for being men! Most men only think about this stuff. Some vent to other men about it, but none of them tell women, because they know it's not politically correct to say any of it out loud.

To understand this male angst, take a few minutes to do the following brief exercise. This enticing activity serves as an ideal beginning before you embark on a complete reading of the book. It's really quite easy. Just fill in the following sentence any way you like. "Forty years ago, a woman did not _____." Take your time and think about it for a few minutes. Have some fun with it. It could even be the theme of a party. Get together with some friends, break out the cheese ball, pour a glass of wine, and generate an exhaustive list. Here are some suggestions to help you get going. Forty years ago, a woman typically did not:

- Call a guy before he called her
- Initiate sex
- Earn her own money
- Have a college degree
- Become the boss at work
- Have her own credit
- Get a car loan or get a mortgage to buy a house on her own
- Participate in the same sports as men
- Portray the role of superhero in a movie
- Enter the military and fight in a war

Forty years ago, working women didn't typically hold professional positions such as doctor, lawyer, accountant, or sales executive, or own their own businesses either. In fact, forty years ago, women would not have had their own careers, anchored the news on television, or been sideline reporters at professional sports events, let alone have their own professional sports leagues. They typically would not have been heads of households, taken their own vacations, or traveled as a part of their work. And they damn sure wouldn't have had tattoos, belly-rings, or those tiny little barbells pierced through their tongues!

Women in America today are doing *all* of these things, and more. To quote a TV commercial from years past, speaking to women as a group, "You've come a long way, baby!" Opportunities for women in education, careers, politics, sports, money, and even sex have increased exponentially since the '60s. And while women have been enjoying these and many other cultural role changes, most men have done nothing but stand by and watch. The more things change, the more some things stay the same. So, *should* a gentleman offer a lady a Tiparillo?

This World Just Isn't Big Enough for the Both of Us!

Would everyone be better off if women and men really did live totally separate lives? There would be no more battle of the sexes. No more gender stereotyping. No more feminist movement. No more male chauvinist pigs. No more spin the bottle, Twister, or sock hops either. Of course that would mean the bon-vivant box-office leading men would be rendered redundant too. No more Brad Pitt, George Clooney, or Pierce Brosnan. *Oceans 1–47*, and the entire James Bond series would likely cease to exist. And imagine Clark Gable in such a world. I guess he'd have no choice but to declare, "Frankly, *Frank*, I don't give a damn!" Oh, the slings and arrows of dramatic dialogue.

But what about sex? Who would men and women be attracted to? Would everyone simply become homosexual? And what about marriage? Maybe women would marry other women, and men would tie the knot with other men. Such a coupling might work, especially if one of them had full dental coverage.

There could be some sort of heterosexual vacation retreat destination where eager participants could meet for a little pleasure in the boudoir. A trendy travel agency could offer eight-days/seven-nights sexy vacation packages to Horneyville. Each trip could include a complimentary split of champagne with chocolate-covered strawberries and a package of ribbed Trojans in every room, all for just $6,969 per person based on double occupancy.

Or could men and women have no real need for sex anymore? Maybe babies really could be delivered by a stork. Better yet, each species could continue in perpetuity by simply ordering the next generation online. In today's high-tech, high-speed, I-can-do-anything-you-can-do world, if sex were no longer a factor in relationships, would women and men really need each other anymore for anything?

Gender roles have become so homogenized that the lines between what is masculine and feminine have been blurred beyond recognition. Some guys actually believe that aside from contributing their seed to propagate the species, there is no utilitarian *need* for them anymore. Men were brought up to be the proverbial knights in shining armor ready to save the damsels in distress. They had a job to do, a role to fill, and women counted on them to do both. But the problem so many men face these days is that they can't find the damsels anymore.

What happened to the days when men were men and women were glad they were? And how do guys *really* feel about how their world has changed? What do they keep hidden in their heads but won't say out loud? And if a guy does say something in the forest and a woman isn't there to hear it, *is* he still wrong? Inquiring minds simply must know.

The Disclaimer

This book is social commentary. The names, ages, locations, and occupations of the people you will read about have all been changed to protect their privacy, and to limit my liability. Yeah, that's right, the classic CYA approach, so I don't have to worry about having my tires slit or waking up some morning with a donkey's ass in my bed.

I have a master's degree in Counseling and Human Development, teach college classes about this stuff, and conducted all the research and interviews that serve as the foundation for this book myself. I am also a baby boomer and have experienced our culture's changing gender roles firsthand. Still, I do not claim to be an expert, nor do I provide any professional advice in any way. If you want help, call Dr. Phil or Jerry Springer.

For your entertainment, I have included my always genuine, sometimes cynical, sometimes humorous, thought-provoking, biting bits of wisdom. I poke fun at both men and women equally, so open your mind to taking all this in under the auspices of having a good time and with the appropriate degree of healthy humility, whether you are a man or a woman, because believe me, there's plenty of material for us to enjoy from both sides.

And if you deem it necessary, consult your therapist before embarking on any undertaking of this nature and know that, though rare, typical side effects may include mild tummy aches from laughing out loud, facial flushing caused by uncovering certain truths about oneself, blurred vision from the occasional tear in the eyes, and, in exceptional cases, actual intellectual and/or emotional epiphanies. Above all, remember, when it comes to men and women and their respective differences, battle of the sexes or not, we're all swimming at our own risk, and there is no lifeguard on duty.

2

WE *HAD* OUR MANHOOD WHEN WE CAME IN HERE!

Once upon a time, in a land far away, where each day slipped peacefully into the next, people lived in a fairy tale. Guys were gallant heroes on the gridiron, and girls were their spirited cheerleaders on the sidelines or doting girlfriends in the stands. Acne-prone teenagers with steamy dreams copped a feel and "made out," for hours, fogging every window in the '58 Oldsmobile while "parking" in a vacant field on the outskirts of town. Men had jobs and paid the bills, while women had children and harried the Hoover. At dinner parties husbands remained at the table with cigars while wives cleaned up and prepared dessert. Life had its routine, and folks lived routine lives.

Then in 1964, it all began to change. Blame it on the Beatles. The Fab Four sported mop tops, which led to the infamous "long-haired hippies." For the first time, women saw another form of humanoid, with flowing long hair and no bra, doing things other than nursing babies and vacuuming the hallway. A light bulb flickered beneath one blonde's highlights; she decided to burn her bra, and the world most men knew and loved would never be the same again.

Four decades have passed since the feminist movement first hit the streets, yet men continue to define their manhood essentially the same three ways: through sex, work, and money. But now men are finding that getting laid, getting made, and getting paid have become more challenging than ever. As a result, most guys are more confused than Gomer Pyle trying to read the seating chart at a Playboy Mansion dinner party!

They still want to have sex, go to work, and earn money, but they're finding themselves having to compete for all three, not only against other men but against *women* too! Many disgruntled men feel it's become the boys against the girls for jobs, money, and especially for sex, since women no longer have to cover up that lovemaking can actually be fun!

A Case of Basic Economics

Economists often say that money is power, and forty years ago in the United States men earned the money, so naturally they had the power. Women typically played the supportive, even subservient role. Single women aspired to meet and marry men who could be good providers. Most of the girls who attended college were there less for the academics than for the pursuit of the coveted "M.R.S." degree, hoping to complete their half of the then-typical and then-prevalent domestic economic equation.

Once married, women relied on their husbands to provide financial support in exchange for a host of routine domestic behaviors dutifully performed on a daily basis to care properly for and sustain the household and family. While their husbands were at work, women prepared the meals, cleaned the house, did the laundry, watched after the kids, and ran errands to the bank, the grocery store, and the dry cleaner. And we wonder why women are better at multitasking.

Those women who were employed outside the home typically held only administrative support positions, such as sales secretary, bookkeeper, or telephone operator. The key jobs, especially the professional and top income-producing positions, belonged to the men, and even job titles were gender-specific such as sales*man*, chair*man*, work*man*, milk*man*, news*man*, or post*man*. As a mid-twentieth-century version of the prehistoric hunters and

8

gatherers, men "hunted" for money while women "gathered" for the family.

Women were also relegated to play supportive roles in the bedroom and were expected to be appropriately accommodating whenever their men wanted or "needed" it. Each particular lady's participation was all but mandatory and necessarily complied with *his* schedule, not hers. Often she acquiesced whenever he wanted it, even if merely in perfunctory fashion, because she felt she had no choice, unless, of course, she could feign the proverbial headache. Not surprisingly, men typically complained they didn't have sex often enough, while women complained they had to have it far too often.

Yes, in the 1950s and early '60s men went to work, earned the money, and controlled the family sex life. Women stayed home endeavoring to both oblige and satisfy their men. A man's home was his castle, and he was its king. And television brought us *Father Knows Best* and *Leave It to Beaver* to model it. Jim Anderson and Ward Cleaver ruled the roost, while Betty and June presided over the kitchen and the cleaning.

Congratulations, you've just completed this special section of History 101—Mid-Century Gender Roles. Thanks for your attendance; we'll send you your diploma next week, as soon as the administrative assistants print them and mail them out. But please be patient, these *guys* don't work as fast as the more adept girls they replaced.

Women, Women, Everywhere!

Fast-forward to the new millennium; oh my, how things have changed. When I wake up every morning, I ask myself four very important questions: Where am I going today? What am I doing? Who am I seeing? And most importantly, do I *really* need to shave? On this particular day, after careful consideration, I decide I can skip using the blade and make my way into the kitchen for a quick breakfast. I take command of the remote—after all, I am a guy—and turn on the TV to catch the local news and get briefed on the forecasted weather. I spot what appears to be a disturbing pattern. On channel eleven there's a woman co-anchor, another woman doing the weather, another woman doing the morning rush-hour traffic report, *another* woman reporting in from the field—and one man as the other co-anchor.

I switch to channel eight, where I see a woman co-anchor, a woman doing the traffic, a woman doing the in-field reporting, a man co-anchor, and lo and behold, another man doing the weather! Next it's down to channel five. A woman as co-anchor, a woman doing the traffic, a woman doing the weather, a woman doing the in-field reporting, and squeezed strategically in between, a man as the other co-anchor. Okay, I'll jump over to channel four. Wow, there's a woman co-anchor, a woman doing the traffic, a woman doing the in-field reporting, a man doing the weather, and—look at that! Another *man* as the co-anchor!

Why are there women, women, everywhere? What happened to the men? I wonder aloud, "Should guys be enraged?" Should men all over America feel persecuted, oppressed by the mainstream majority? Could there actually be a Plexiglas ceiling in the television news business? Even perennial cutie Katie Couric is now anchoring the *CBS Evening News*, the first woman ever in that job. But before that, at NBC, she was paid more money than her co-anchor Matt Lauer. What about equal pay for equal work? Did Katie do more work than Matt?

Shouldn't guys be *really* upset about this? In the ongoing battle of the sexes, it seems the WACs have hunkered down into the men's barracks and started claiming squatters' rights! Somebody better do something fast. Maybe it's time for a masculinist movement. Maybe some guy somewhere needs to burn his jock and declare war against women. Then again, maybe it's just the way of the world. I'll think about it, but right now I'm going to keep flipping back and forth between channel eleven and channel eight. Those women are freakin' HOT!

Maybe It's the Thought That Counts

Many women claim that men think about only one thing—sex! Believe it or not, such a statement is patently false. Men think about work and money too, especially about how they can *work* to make the *money* they can use to get the *sex*! But to be fair, many men claim that women, too, think about only one thing—how to change men! This statement is also patently false. Women think about work and money too. Especially about how they can *work* to make the *money* they can use to become *self-sufficient* so their men have no choice but to change!

But men do not change quickly or easily. As women's roles have evolved, some guys appear oblivious to accepting them as equals. Others of an egalitarian mind understand and willingly embrace the enhanced opportunities for women. But almost *all* men really wish women would get a better handle on the extent to which they've been affected by how dramatically women's roles have changed.

What's a Man to Do?

According to the U.S. Census Bureau, there are an estimated seventy-eight million baby boomers, and approximately 49 percent of them are men. That means there are some thirty-eight million guys out there who share a similar belief that their primary roles in life are to perform the three Ps: Provide, Protect, and Procreate. As women continue to prove they can accomplish all three without men, literally millions of men in America, even four decades into the shifting gender role paradigm, find themselves in a quandary about how to revise their definition of manhood. They keep asking themselves, "What's a man do to?"

Legions of beleaguered men are scrambling to adjust to a new world where women are doctors, lawyers, accountants, and leaders in the corporate workplace. There are women working professionally as officials in the NBA, sideline reporters in the NFL, and sportscasters reporting results in Major League Baseball. Even Annika Sörenstam competed in a PGA event!

Men see women playing what were traditionally men's sports, besting men in physical fights in the movies, and being portrayed as the smart ones in television sitcoms. Some are even initiating sex! And nubile young ladies are wearing men's clothes, driving military-class Humvees, and sporting tattoos, belly rings, and combat boots. Many of them look like they could check either box on an employment application where it asks for the person's gender. And by the way, what's up with these unisex bathrooms?

Most men are not coming forward to share their opinions and concerns, and their silence makes sense when viewed from a cultural perspective. Men have been taught since they were little boys that it is not manly to disclose fears and worries or to show vulnerability or concern. They were also taught not to compete against girls, and above all else to remember, "Big boys don't cry!" Again, they also know it's politically incorrect to speak out.

While the enactment of such egalitarian endeavors as the Equal Pay Act, Title IX, and affirmative action have helped women take great strides forward, many men continue to be baffled by it all. They understand both how and why women's roles have changed, but they're struggling to make sense out of how and where they fit in. Often at home, unemployed, and feeling inadequate as providers, they are also fast losing confidence in their ability to protect.

When these two traditional roles, provider and protector, have been quelled or suppressed, leaving men feeling less important to the survival and safety of women, it may also adversely affect an even more potent measure of their manhood—their confidence as sexual beings. Stripping men of their roles as providers and protectors can, in their minds, threaten their roles as procreators, and as a result, render them nearly impotent in all three.

Women's attitudes toward men have changed too. Should a well-meaning swain open a door for a woman today, she'll insist she's self-sufficient. But should he *fail* to open the same door for the same woman, she'll accuse him of not treating her like a lady. If a guy offers to pick up the check at dinner, all too often the girl tells him she can pay for herself. But if he fails to ante up, she'll brand him as cheap and scratch him from her list of "ADCs," Acceptable Date Candidates. Men think chivalry hasn't died, only to discover they've spread their shirts across the puddle for a whole new species of "fair ladies" they've never encountered before.

A lot of men claim they *had* their manhood when they came into this party called life but can't seem to find it amid all of these new age, tenacious, competitive chicks who can match them point for point, tit for tat. Women have become superpowers in the business world, supermoms at home, superstars in sports, and thanks to the marvels of modern medical procedures, as hot as supermodels everywhere else. And while all of this may be both long overdue and celebrated on behalf of women, it has many men feeling more challenged than Howard Stern hosting *The 700 Club*.

Out of the Mouths of Men

Jerry, fifty-two, a contractor from Scottsdale, Arizona, says he is confused when he meets with a female client. "I was brought up to shake hands with men, not with women. With women you just nod or bow your head slightly, or take their hands very lightly for a few seconds and that's it. But now when I meet a woman the first time at a job site or in the office, a lot of them grab my hand and shake it like a man would. I don't really like that. Women are supposed to be feminine."

Max, forty-seven, a department-store manager from Detroit, Michigan, agrees. "Yeah, it's really confusing. I don't know whether to shake a woman's hand or not anymore, and if I do, I don't know how. Are we supposed to shake their hands with a firm, tight grip or with a soft, loose grip? Worse than that, I've actually had some women tell me I'm being disrespectful to them if I don't shake their hand firmly, and then others tell me they don't like a man to do that, so how the hell can we win anymore?"

Lowell, a sixty-one-year-old retired draftsman from Hobbs, New Mexico, thinks chivalry may have gone by the wayside. "I like to open a door for a woman. It doesn't matter if it is a door to a building or the car door, and it doesn't matter if it is a woman I'm with or even a total stranger. I just like to do it because I've always thought that's what a thoughtful man does for a woman. But the other day I tried to open the door to an art gallery for a woman coming in just behind me, and she stopped right then and there and told me she could open it herself. Since when is doing something nice for another human being considered an insult?"

And Pete, forty-nine, an optometrist from Little Rock, Arkansas, says he got scolded one night for asking the woman he was dining with if she wanted to split the check. "I've always assumed that when I'm out with a woman I'm supposed to pay the check, and I like it that way. But I've had more than one dinner companion tell me she wanted to pay her share. So when I was out the other night with a friend of mine and asked her if she wanted to split the check, she really got upset and bitched at me that I was cheap and needed to get real and be a man! The next time I go out, what should I do? It seems if I try to pay, they think I'm showing off, but if I ask them for any money, I'm not being a man. I just wish women would make up their minds which way they want to go with all of this battle-of-the-sexes stuff. Is it supposed to be the old way or the new way? I just don't get it, and I'm getting to the point where I really am losing interest in even getting together with them. If I go have dinner with one of my buddies, he'll just pay his share, and I don't have to second-guess anybody."

A *Men's* Movement?

So is it time for a masculinist movement? Some people say it is, a time for men to reclaim and reassert their masculinity. But writers such as Robert Bly, Sam Keen, Robert Moore, Douglas Gillette and others already tried to jump-start a men's movement in the early 1990s. Men went out into the woods clad in loin cloths, beat drums, howled at the moon, and then "shared their feelings" with one another while sitting in circles, naked, sequestered for hours in sweat lodges.

The idea was to get in touch with the wild men residing deep within them, suppressed into hiding by an industrialized nation that rewarded gender homogeneity. The goal was to reassert the industry and strength of manliness and masculinity. Men needed time together, away from women, so they could individuate from the "mother" figure in their lives and celebrate the ancient rites and rituals of traditional manhood. The movement disintegrated faster than a snowman in a steam bath. And while the men were out bonding, sweating their salamis off in the wilderness, women were successfully charging the castle, capturing the adolescent sentries standing guard, and changing the locks on the drawbridges.

The *Housekeeping Monthly* Girls

Allegedly, in 1955, in its May 13 issue, *Housekeeping Monthly* magazine printed what they called "The Good Wife's Guide." I say allegedly, because the authenticity of the piece cannot be verified.

Some believe it was merely a hoax, but the alleged article looks quite real and today can be found making its way around the world from one e-mail address to the next. Eighteen specific bullet points were listed to provide women with expert guidance on "how to be a good wife." I've gleaned what a group of us voted were the top ten tips in the article and include them here for your thoughtful consideration and unending entertainment. I've taken the liberty to italicize some of the more potent points. After you read the list in its entirety, go through it a second time reading only the italicized words, to get the full, rather eye-opening effect.

1. *Have dinner ready.* Plan ahead, even the night before, to have a delicious meal ready, on time for his return. This is a way of letting him know that you've been thinking about him and are concerned about his needs.

2. Prepare yourself. Take fifteen minutes to rest so you'll be refreshed when he arrives. *Touch up your makeup, put a ribbon in your hair, and be fresh-looking. He has just been with a lot of work-weary people.*

3. Clear away the clutter. Make one last trip through the main part of the house just before your husband arrives.

4. Over the cooler months of the year, you should prepare and light a fire for him to unwind by. Your husband will feel he has reached a haven of rest and order, and it will give you a lift too. After all, *catering for his comfort will provide you with immense personal satisfaction.*

5. Greet him with a warm smile, and *show sincerity in your desire to please him.*

6. Listen to him. You may have a dozen important things to tell him, but the moment of his arrival is not the time. *Let him talk first—remember, his topics of conversation are more important than yours.*

7. Make the evening his. *Never complain if he comes home late or goes out to dinner or other places of entertainment without you.* Instead, try to understand his world of strain and pressure and his very real need to be at home and relax.

8. *Don't complain if he's late home for dinner or even if he stays out all night.* Count this as minor compared to what he might have gone through that day.

9. *Don't ask him questions about his actions or question his judgment or integrity.* Remember, he *is the master of the house* and as such will always exercise his will with fairness and truthfulness. *You have no right to question him.*

10. *A good wife always knows her place.*

And we wonder why men aren't exactly hauling ass to sign up for the new-millennium way of life. If there are any women out there who truly believe in these tips, please e-mail me right away at iwantyounowandwillkeepyouforeverandgiveyoueverythinginmywill.com.

If the twenty-first century version of this same article were printed today, it might read something like this. Once again, key points are in italics.

1. *Call him on your cell phone or text message him to see* if he is going to get home before you do, and ask him *if he will have dinner ready.* Plan ahead, even the night before. If you already know you don't want to eat at home, decide where you're

going to enjoy a delicious meal, and let him know he is free to join you if he so desires. This is a way of letting him know that you've been thinking about him and are concerned about his needs.

2. Prepare yourself. Get there fifteen minutes early and have a drink so you'll be ready to act interested in him when he arrives. *Touch up your makeup and your hair so you can look good at the bar* while you wait for him. Remember, he knows that you, like all of the other beautiful people at the bar, spent the day with a lot of work-weary souls.

3. Ignore the clutter just as he does. And over the cooler months of the year, you should encourage him to stock plenty of firewood so that he can light a fire you can both unwind by. Your husband will feel he has reached a haven of rest and order once he's finished stacking the wood, and it will give you a lift too. After all, *since you also have a career, allowing him to procure the wood will help safeguard his need to feel manly and will provide you with immense personal satisfaction.*

4. Greet him with a warm smile and *show sincerity in your desire to be pleased by him*, and be sure to remind him how well he's doing relative to the quota you've established for your lovemaking.

5. Listen to him. You may have a dozen important things to tell him, but he can't multitask like you can, so *let him talk first—remember, his topics of conversation are far less important than yours, so get them out of the way before you begin.*

6. Make the evening his and yours. Never complain if he comes home late or goes out to dinner or other places of entertainment without you. Instead, *you too can come home late or go out to dinner or other places of entertainment without him.* Help him try to understand his world of strain and pressure is no different from yours, just as his very real need to be at home and relax is likewise the same as yours.
7. Don't complain if he's late for dinner or even if he stays out all night. *Count this as minor compared to the punishment you will dole out when he does get home*, and to hell with what he might have gone through that day.
9. Don't ask him questions about his actions or question his judgment or integrity. Remember, he's just a guy and will screw up again and again. *You are the mistress of the house,* and as such will always exercise your will with fairness and truthfulness. And remember, *he has no right to question you about anything. After all, you have been unjustly oppressed for fifty-four long years since we ran that ridiculous article back in 1955!*
10. *A good wife always knows her place—FIRST PLACE!*

That's Just Not Fair!

From the late fifties through the seventies, men witnessed June Cleaver morph into Mary Tyler Moore. By the eighties she had become Murphy Brown, and by the turn of the century even that famous feme sole transitioned into Carrie Bradshaw. A lot of men today feel that women have been given an advantage over them. They realize that the long-standing roles and rules that served to delineate clearly what constitutes acceptable behavior for men and women have changed. But no one has told them what their revised roles are, how to fit in, or where they belong. Is all really fair in love and war?

Bill, fifty-five, a former sales manager from Albuquerque, New Mexico, worked at one of America's largest corporations until he and a female co-worker both lost their jobs. "I worked at that company for seven years, and I watched them terminate a woman who was barely over forty and had worked there the same length of time I did. It took nine months, a file on the woman that was more than two inches thick, and a six-figure severance check before they could get rid of her. It took fifteen minutes and only the standard severance check to fire me, and we both had the same tenure with the company and were terminated for exactly the same reasons."

Roger, forty-one, a warehouse supervisor from Boston, Massachusetts, thinks it's unfair to charge men a cover charge at bars while letting the women in for free. "Why do they have what they call 'ladies' nights' but they never have any 'men's nights?' I mean, fair is fair. If women get in for free, men should too. Better yet, if men have to pay, women should have to pay too."

Kevin, forty-four, a CPA from Queens, New York, says it used to be a man's world but not anymore. "For decades we've been told it's a man's world. Is it? No doubt it used to be. It definitely was in the '50s and '60s, but is it truly a man's world today? I think NOT!"

Maybe women should start opening doors for men. They could also start handling the driving and paying for some dinners too. Maybe it's time women really got on top both figuratively and literally. Or have they already achieved that? Maybe men and women really *would* be better off if they lived on separate planets. Hey, look at it optimistically. We wouldn't have to worry about those confounded unisex bathrooms.

Women Too?

Paradoxically, scores of women are also confused. They're trying to exploit new opportunities available to them today that their mothers never had. But they also want to selectively retain certain preferred characteristics attributed to the more traditionally feminine roles. Many of them in their late thirties and early forties have college degrees, earn six figures in professional positions, dress in the latest fashions, and drive the hottest cars but wonder why they don't have a husband, a house with a white picket fence, and two perfect children.

Untold numbers of women are asking, "Whose idea was this anyway?" They're questioning the possible side effects, the contraindications of the new paradigm for women they bought into decades earlier, while experiencing a void deep within their relational makeup that yearns to be filled. And for many of them—though their noses may still tilt slightly up in the air—they're no longer pulling in the fragrance of feministic arrogance, but rather sniffing for the once-familiar scent of a man.

Regardless of the redolence of flying pheromones at the local meat market, there are still many women out there who want the check paid and the door opened for them. These ladies know that though the sisterhood is better able than ever to "bring home the bacon and fry it up in the pan," they may have unwittingly misplaced what it takes to "never let him forget he's a man!" Indeed, if a man's home was once his castle, for many a man in the new millennium, his manhood has somehow found its way into the moat.

Many women are discovering that Mr. Right is fast becoming an endangered species. Though still very much on the lookout for him, they're having a hard time pinpointing his precise whereabouts. Make no mistake about it, women still want men. They may complain about the lazy couch potatoes, but most women would rather have some fat waste of space belching on the Barcalounger than to stare into a conspicuously empty living room. They enjoy having their own personal piñata with a penis, and don't forget: they still need somebody to take out the trash.

What's a Guy to Do?

Many men feel as if they fell into a deep sleep at the end of the '60s, woke up in the twenty-first century, and found that women had pulled off a collective extreme makeover—species edition—while they were away.

Somewhere along the line the gender game changed, and now most women measure off the charts in self-sufficiency. It's a whole new world indeed, and a world that at times doesn't seem to have room for traditional men. It's no wonder some men can't get a homeless girl even if they offer her a free home.

Many men feel relationship-challenged. Some of them so much so they may actually qualify for preferred parking. Of course they have secrets about this stuff. Is that so surprising? Without a doubt, men have secrets. They just keep them inside the clubhouse.

Sex

"Hi, I'm Liz . . . you'll do."

3

ELECTRICAL PLUGS AND WALL SOCKETS

Secret No. 1:
"Women should play the hunted, not the hunter."

Meet Rusty, a thirty-nine-year-old journeyman electrician from Cleveland, Ohio. He is one of America's proud working class and fits the quintessential image of the traditional macho man. Rusty played football in high school, chased cheerleaders behind the bleachers, and subscribed to the old adage, "Real men don't eat quiche!" But lately it seems he's having trouble dealing with women he thinks are too sexually aggressive.

"I'm a man's man, and I'm used to making the first move when I'm with a woman. That's the way it's supposed to be, isn't it? But now, I go out with a girl for the first time, and when we get back to her place, she starts pushing *me* to get naked! It freaks me out because I'm not used to that, and because it can be humiliating if I'm not, well, you know, ready yet." Then he leaned toward me and whispered, "It's tough to get it up when she's being so aggressive like that. It's a whole lot easier when I know what to expect, when *I* control the game."

Don, forty-seven, a business manager from Los Angeles, California, agrees. "The game has really changed. I used to know how to play it, [and] so did everyone else, the guys and the girls. The guy asked the girl out, and the guy was the one who made the first move. I never have a problem when I call the shots, but when a woman starts jumping my bones before I make my first move, I don't like it. It just doesn't seem right to me."

Is this how most men feel? Or are Rusty and Don just a couple of old-school guys? Maybe Rusty, given that he's an electrician, believes that when it comes to sex, a man and a woman should be just like an electrical plug and a wall socket. The plug is supposed to slide into the socket, not the other way around. I must admit, I've never actually seen a wall socket jump on a plug first, but I can see where it could be a real problem for the plug.

Rusty and Don do make a good point. Many women are no longer willing to wait for men to initiate; they eagerly anticipate having sex. As they hone in on a desirable partner, some of them can be more aggressive than Courtney Love in the piano bar at the Waldorf. This particular sex role reversal has caught many men by surprise, leaving them feeling quite vulnerable, and often causing them to second-guess their natural instincts.

When it comes to sex, Secret No. 1 that men think but don't tell women is, *"Women should play the hunted, not the hunter."* Men have been hunters since prehistoric times. They've been taking the lead in the bedroom for just as long. Expecting them to reverse a protocol that's been in existence since human life began in as little as one or two generations is a tall order. Most of them haven't learned how to cook a frozen pizza yet.

Greg, fifty-three, a banker from Brooklyn, New York, says if you take away the hunt, he's no longer interested. "I like a girl who wants to be pursued. I love the little cat and mouse games we can play, but most of all I want to do the chasing because I feel like more of a man when I do. If a woman comes on too strong, it turns me off. I want to pursue her. I don't like it the other way around."

Rusty, Don, and Greg believe men should signal when it's time for sex. But is that really fair? Wouldn't it make sense that they'd be enjoying it more often if the women could initiate too? Were women to beckon a bounce in the buff, why wouldn't men welcome the opportunity with, shall we say, more than just open arms?

Of course, some men do. Steve, a single, fifty-year-old executive from Chicago, Illinois, is one such guy. "I love it when women initiate sex, even in a bar. The world is different than it was in the seventies. Women are stronger than they used to be, and they want everything RFF (real freaking fast)! A guy should be secure enough in his masculinity that a woman hitting on him doesn't bother him."

Luke, a thirty-five-year-old personal trainer from Pennsylvania, agrees. "Yeah, I like it when a woman hits on me. I'm a trainer, so I've got the body, and I know how to use it. It's cool with me if they tell me they want sex. As far as I'm concerned, it's easier for me that way. I can get what I want without having to put in the usual effort it takes to get it."

Still, most guys agree with Rusty and Don and are uncomfortable when a woman makes the first move. Ken, a single, forty-one-year-old landscape architect from Riviera Beach, Florida, said he gets nervous when a woman presses him to have sex. "I don't like it at all. It goes against everything I believe about men and women. Put it this way, I like to lead when I dance."

Tony, fifty-eight, a wholesale distributor from Brooklyn, New York, added, "My wife and I will be married thirty-three years next month, and she never tries to get me to have sex. She hints at it sometimes, and, if I'm in the mood, we'll do it. But I can tell you this, if I don't want to do it, it isn't going to happen. I'm the one who gets that ball rolling."

Andrew, forty-nine, a dentist from Fort Lauderdale, Florida, says he's hardwired to be the hunter. "I don't want women to be aggressive and make the first move even to *meet* me, much less tell me they want sex. I would be totally intimidated if a woman started playing grab-ass with me in front of a bunch of people at a party or in a bar. I like to be in control of what I do, and I prefer women that want it that way too."

Why do some men struggle with women initiating sex while others welcome it? Could it be as Steve suggests? Do men just need to be more secure with their masculinity? Most men want to feel virile, potent, and heroic to women. In their minds, when women lead the charge toward a sexual conquest, they leave their femininity scattered across the floor along the same path to the bedroom as their clothes.

Wade, forty-seven, an entrepreneur from Orlando, Florida, understands his brothers' angst. "My first reaction when you told me women are initiating sex was 'Bring it on baby!' But I'll tell you this: When I'm in a bar, I'm on the prowl, and I think most guys will agree it just isn't the same gig when it's the other way around. I want to be in charge, at least in the beginning, you know, during what I like to call "The Hunt." After that, once we've consummated the relationship, it doesn't really matter anymore. I can see what Rusty's talking about, and I have to admit, I agree."

But can't guys simply say no? Just as women have the right to refuse when men want to have sex, if women choose to initiate when they're interested, men have the right to say no, too. Some women are simply more sexually aggressive than others, and today they are much freer to express their desire and interest than they ever could have forty years ago. Any guy not interested in a woman who takes a proactive approach to expressing her sexual manifest destiny can simply refuse to play.

Guys who find life on the sexual superhighway a bit too much might think about getting out of the fast lane and pulling into the nearest rest stop. They can simply take a breather and be comfortable with their own sexuality. And if all else fails, they can always wear a turtleneck and a chastity belt until they're ready.

Generally speaking, men have no problem with women initiating sex once a couple has established a sex life together. But in the beginning, men want to be the hunters doing the pursuing, and the women they find most attractive, even alluring, are the ones who want to be hunted, to be pursued. Men like women who want to be chased.

Most men might never admit it out loud, but it's no coincidence that Sally Field, Meg Ryan, Julia Roberts, Sandra Bullock, and more recently, Kate Hudson and Jennifer Aniston have often been called, "America's Sweethearts." These women all share at least one thing in common: they have an established image as "good girls." Marilyn Monroe may have been the first-ever centerfold for *Playboy* magazine, but Audrey Hepburn was the girl most guys imagined taking home to meet their mothers.

Men may talk a good game, but they would never sign up to play the entrée de jour in an episode of *Mutual of Omaha's Wild Kingdom*. Plant a buxom blonde on the barstool next to a guy, her room key falling out of her cleavage as she downs a shot of Louis, squeezes his inner thigh, winks and turns to leave. He'll buddy up to the dude sitting to his right faster than Don Imus at a Rutger's University women's basketball game.

Smart women know what men really want when it comes to initiating sex. They understand how the sexual safari works, especially the go-away-a-little-closer game. They also know how to play the hunt*ed*. And they execute it flawlessly until they've captured their prey.

4

POCKET ROCKETS AND PERFORMANCE ANXIETY

Secret No. 2: "Women should be *assertive* . . . not aggressive."

What is the real dynamic at play here? Is it that women are being too aggressive, or that men simply want to be aggressive first? Could it be a performance issue, or is it simply a challenge to the male ego? Maybe there is some deep-seated psychological dynamic at play. A subconscious psychosexual inadequacy awakened by the role reversal, exposing some form of latent femininity in men. Or maybe they just don't look good in a camisole and a pair of heels.

Performance Anxiety? Me?

Most men tend to find it difficult to respond to women who take a more aggressive approach to sex. Could guys like Rusty and Don be suffering from performance anxiety? Perish the thought that their pocket rockets might "not be ready yet." More importantly, these two are not isolated cases. Untold numbers of men across America collectively share their apprehension but are doing so in, shall we say, silent withdrawal.

This problem appears to be especially true for men in their forties and beyond who believe they are supposed to take the lead in a sexual relationship. When women play what has traditionally been the masculine role, it turns most men off. Guys would feel more comfortable in a bull ring with a slingshot than in the bedroom with some brunette bombshell charging at them, waving her copy of the *Kama Sutra* and yelling, "I want to do the Lotus-like position . . . NOW!"

Baby Boomers were raised to believe that a man is supposed to be a woman's knight in shining armor, the cock of the walk, the victor over all others who are likewise allured by her charms. And a woman is supposed to be his adoring fair maiden. Both were oriented to believe that a couple's sexual activity should happen at the behest of the male, with the female only too happy to oblige. Less-compliant women who saw pleasing their men as nothing more than perfunctory duty simply learned to fabricate reasons to abstain, such as, "Not tonight, honey, I have a headache."

But now, legions of men continue to report feeling under attack by a militia of sexually aggressive women advancing faster than K-Mart shoppers at a blue-light special. The behavior of these promiscuous paramours is scrambling the cognitive circuitry in men's brains. When women take charge in the bedroom, many men find themselves feeling less than knightly, figuratively meandering about aimlessly, wondering who stole their horses and protective breastplates.

The New Definition of Sex

A former president of the United States, albeit unwittingly, may have helped fuel this radical evolution of both social and sexual behavior. The mating game changed dramatically after Slick Willie declared, "I did not have sexual relations with that woman!" Ever since he claimed that oral stimulation was nonsexual behavior, whippersnappers as young as fifth and sixth graders across America have been going trouser-trout fishing in Lake Levis because they don't believe they're having sex! These kids figure, "Hey, if the president of the United States can do it, so can we!" What a role model. He may have single-handedly brought a whole new meaning to the term "figurehead"!

Those whippersnappers in elementary and junior high school in the late nineties are now young adults. They are also big sisters and role models for the next generation of sexual beings. Clinton's behavior may well have influenced an overhauling of social and sexual mores. Oh well, who would have expected him to think about that when he decided to administer his infamous oral exam to Monica Lewinsky?

History may show that the greatest contribution Mr. Hillary Clinton made to humankind was the development of a new paradigm for going to first base. But come on, folks, it's not *all* his fault, is it? With all due respect to our former president, Mr. "I feel your pain!" hasn't single-handedly revamped the very meaning of sex. Has he? No doubt he had his hand in there somewhere, but that's a whole separate issue we won't get into here.

But since Mr. Clinton's indiscretion, long-held conventions regarding sexual behavior have evaporated, and much of mainstream America has redefined and narrowed the actual definition of sex to *the act of intercourse*. All other behaviors are just considered good fun, and sexual activity itself has become so casual and permissive that even chance couples meet, get it on, and thereafter simply refer to each other as *friends with benefits*.

Whether such behavior is moral or not isn't the point of this discourse. Though there may be nothing inherently wrong with *fwb*, most guys still want the girls to play along at an appropriate pace. Men don't mind women making sexual advances, regardless of what base they're attempting to steal. They just want them to do it less aggressively.

But being aggressive is not the same as being *assertive*. My research indicates a woman gracefully asserting her interest in sex comes across to a guy as much more palatable than a woman he perceives is aggressively trying to seize and conquer him. Ted, a single, fifty-one-year-old insurance salesman from Tempe, Arizona, succinctly describes the difference in his mind. "Being assertive doesn't make her a bad person, but if she's too aggressive she's like a slut in my mind. I think I speak for a lot of guys when I say that women who are too aggressive can turn guys off because they force us to shift into a defensive mode."

Secret No. 2 that men think but don't tell women is, *"Women should be assertive . . . not aggressive."* When a woman is too aggressive for a man, she lessens the odds of getting what she wants. If she does get what she wants, it will likely be at his expense, leaving him unsatisfied and possibly even intimidated by her advances. Worse, such an offensive approach may turn the guy off. If that happens, it also lessens the odds for a rain check.

By contrast, if she is assertive when communicating her desire for sex, she greatly increases the odds of getting what she wants. He is comfortable with the approach and willingly reciprocates. She gets what she wants, and he gets what he wants. It's a quid pro quo arrangement, or in lay terms, *each* player enjoys a happy ending.

I asked a lot of men exactly what they mean when they say they don't like sexually aggressive women. Clay, forty-seven, a network administrator from Redmond, Washington, may have hit the nail on the head. "I don't like feeling vulnerable and out of control. When a woman is too aggressive I lose interest real fast. I'll tell you about an actual experience I had. I met a hot girl at my gym one night and took her out for dinner. We were having a great time until I dropped her off back at her car and she started pawing me all over my body right there in the parking lot and told me she wanted to throw me into her car, lock the doors, and tear off all of my clothes. I immediately stepped back, told her I had a very early meeting the next morning, and split as fast as I could. She was just too aggressive, and that killed the whole deal for me."

The Temporary Abstinence Movement

As a by-product of, maybe even a backlash to, such behavior by these sexually fearless women, a new men's movement appears to be emerging. *Guys* have started making conscious choices to wear heavy-duty grommet-fly jeans, cross their legs, and say no to sex! Preliminary reconnaissance indicates this movement, now in its seminal stage, could set the dating game on its ear.

Frustrated guys are pulling a behavioral about-face when confronted by one of these confident, new age huntresses who believes *she's* the fastest cheetah on the Discovery Channel. I've pinned my own label on it and call it the Temporary Abstinence Movement, or TAM for short. TAM is a growing fraternity of disillusioned guys who are figuratively pulling back and zipping up because being tagged as the hunt*ed* rather than as the hunt*er* terrifies them.

This female-in-charge-in-the-bedroom gig represents a new standard many men are simply not prepared to accept. Such untraditional behavior is alarming to men, catching them off their guard. For many of them, it's sending Mr. Wiggly into hiding faster than Richard Simmons in cell block nine at San Quentin. And as every guy who has made it through puberty knows, if Mr. Wiggly retreats, it better be because it's freaking cold outside and he's got to fumble around down there just to find it before he can take a leak.

In direct response, many of the more traditional squires are making a rather newfangled decision regarding the old one-night stand. They're refusing to have sex with a woman on the first date, and in many cases are abstaining substantially beyond date No. 1! They're actually keeping their Little Prince Willies sequestered for more than one night before letting them out of their cages to perform their usual carnival acts of carnality. Gee, could this be a case of haste makes chaste?

Women who take advantage of this secret know to advance, but do so with *feminine* charm. Men simply want women to soften their approach. Guys love it when girls openly communicate about what they want, and it can even fuel how the guys respond. But the key for men is *how* the girls communicate. Saying something like, "I love being with you, Bill; I feel so good when we're together. Maybe it would be fun to try the Lotus-like position this time. Are you up for that?" works a lot better for most guys. "Bend over and crack a smile, leave your pants on the floor, and get in here!" is a little much.

Whether or not they admit it out loud, it is a bit of culture shock for most men when they find themselves on the receiving end of an aggressive woman's sexual advances. They're much more comfortable with women who are a little softer and yet assertive in their approach. This isn't to suggest they couldn't eventually adjust to it. In time they can even grow to love it, but they need to be weaned out of the old world and into the new.

Remember, guys need ease and simplicity, orderliness and predictability. We're talking about the phylum of human being that doesn't ask for directions or read the instructions when the box says, "Some assembly required!"

5

PENIS RECON

Secret No. 3: "Don't test for the erection!"

Like those cheetahs on the Discovery Channel, women are not only fast, they're cunning. They're watching these guys. Women are nothing if not observant. The most astute of them are beginning to realize they may be catching guys by surprise and may need to temper their approach to sexual fulfillment—to back off just a bit. One carefully executed brush of her forearm across his pants while they're playing tonsil hockey on the couch can determine whether his woodpecker has flown south for the winter.

The Third-Date Phenomenon

Women know that a southward bird is as good as no bird at all, so many of them on a quest to bed a man have developed a new protocol to follow, one that has become part and parcel of their modern-day dating scene. It is commonly referred to as the third-date phenomenon. These particular women afford the guys three dates before requiring them to serve up the family jewels for the queen's personal pleasure.

Date No. 1 is for drinks over dinner, a few laughs, and of course, the qualification process. For some women, this is the time to get answers to specific questions such as, "What does he do? How much does he make? Where does he live?" Others may even ask, "Who does he know? And what can he do for me?"

Date No. 2 provides further opportunity to socialize and decide whether she thinks he's an okay guy, worthy of some quality time in the sack. This is the time to determine if he's a nice guy or a potential axe murderer.

Date No. 3 is the magical one. That's when Mr. Wiggly is summoned up, even obligated, to make the scene, where casual friendship transcends into casual sex. And if for any reason it doesn't happen on the third date, with rare exception given to a fourth and final chance, these women conclude it simply isn't meant to be with this particular guy and it's time to move on. Or they assume his abstinence is the harbinger for some hidden secret such as, "He must be gay."

By contrast, other women define the third-date phenomenon as the complete opposite. For them the first three dates, while understandably meant for getting to know guys better, are actually the ones used to hold the guys off before *letting* them have sex. They may have just as much interest in enjoying a bounce in the buff as their sisterly cohorts, but choose to be more comfortable with each partner before letting him have what they believe is his target objective. For these girls, it's less about seeking sex and more about pacing when and with whom they allow it. They still want the sex, and they are just as willing to have it on the third date.

As one might expect, most men favor the latter of the two modus operandi because it affords them the role of the hunter, since they are the ones advancing the carnal proposition. But when these guys encounter the former, it is alarming to them, and they find themselves retreating into unfamiliar terrain. They're not used to women *expecting* sex, or having women consider it as routine as having a drink or catching a movie.

It's one thing if the guys expect it; that's the way it's always been. But when it is expected *of* them, it can be more difficult to handle than one might assume. Rusty told me about one girl he dated four times over a two-week period. Upon returning to her apartment late in the evening on the fourth date, after a goodnight kiss, he started to leave. She threw up her arms in frustration and bitched, "What's going on here? By now couples are sleeping with each other!"

The real problem for Rusty and guys like him is not the sexual activity so early in the evolution of a prospective relationship, but the fact that the women are the ones pushing for consummation. It is the role reversal that has guys so screwed up.

Though many of the patriarchal protocols of American society are finally disappearing, most men still want to believe that the conventions regarding sexual behavior will be the last to go. They've come to terms with women earning their own college degrees, securing gainful employment, making their own money, assuming executive roles in the business world, even becoming superheroes on the big screen. But taking the lead sexually? Leading on the sexual dance floor, too? And taking command of the one-night stand, even if it takes three dates to get there? Chester Riley said it best when he proclaimed, "What a revoltin' development *this* is!"

A guy picks up a girl for a first date; they go to dinner, enjoy some small talk, maybe a dance or two. Later at her place, he's invited inside and fills two wine glasses with a trendy chardonnay while she slips into something more comfortable. After she jumps his bones on the couch and plays the French version of post office for a bit, she aggressively jettisons her britches and starts to climb aboard. He notices his space shuttle isn't assuming the usual blast-off position just yet and kills the countdown. "Houston, we have a problem!"

He politely declines, while extending his warmest regrets. Yes, he turns her down! The guy's plug is simply not accustomed to being jumped by a wall socket it barely knows, and he can't help but feel the shortcoming deep within his demilitarized zone. He thought it was supposed to be the other way around. He thought *he* would be slipping *his* plug into *her* socket as soon as he could grab hold of the stiff cord!

To avoid any further humiliation, he whips out his TAM membership card, proudly displays it to her, thanks her for a wonderful evening, and utters those infamous last words, "I'll call you!" He's off to see the wizard for more than a new brain and some much-needed courage. He's carrying his American TAM card, and he's learned never to leave home without it.

Alien Beavers in Uncharted Waters

More men than might be expected are holding off awhile longer before throwing Mr. Wiggly into uncharted waters where alien beavers have been known to appear without warning. More wary than ever of jumping in bed with someone they just met an hour or two ago, they too are practicing members of the TAM. But why the sudden about-face by these guys?

Here's one theory, postulated after years of exhaustive research and analysis, as well as a few close encounters with those alien beavers. It's really quite simple, and in fact, Rusty is more in tune with all of this than he thinks. Regarding sexual intercourse, biologically speaking, women are the receiving end of the connection. Anatomically speaking, the vagina is the receptacle, the opening into which the penis enters. Like the simple electrical outlet on the wall, its role is clearly one of hosting, harboring, providing anchorage, a port, a haven, *a landing place for the plug.*

Just as a train must travel *into* a tunnel, or an electrical plug must be inserted *into* an outlet, the penis must somehow make its way *into* the vagina. Whether entrance is achieved using the traditional missionary position with the male on top, with the female taking the lead and proficiently lowering herself onto her partner, or any other of the many positions available, the penis must nonetheless make its entry. To do so successfully it must be in the requisite state of tumescence, the readiness commonly referred to as the erection, the boner, the hard-on.

In more simplistic terms, in order for the guy to be able to get it in, he has to be able to get it *up* first. And although women possess motility the common wall socket is without, they can no more proactively descend upon a flaccid Mr. Wiggly than a frolicking tomboy upon a deflated beach ball. That said, men want women to understand that executing a sexual surprise attack on an unwitting guy may be all it takes to flatten his inflatable.

Ideally, a couple engaging in a sexual union creates a loving, perhaps even symbiotic relationship, with each person providing satisfaction for the other. But he must be in a state of readiness to accomplish the mission. And though she does too, she doesn't have to wear hers, or lack thereof, like a Ralph Lauren logo on her person for all to see. He does. If he's not up for the job, everyone in the room knows it.

Many women have been quick to suggest that sex isn't all about the erection anyway. They remind men that there are a number of ways to pleasure a woman other than with a stiff penis. Guys know that, girls; they've also heard that size is no indication of performance. That must explain why women at those bachelorette parties focus exclusively on the stripper's face and wonderful personality.

Most men are aware that women can be turned on and sexually satisfied through methods of lovemaking other than, or in addition to, intercourse. Still, every guy believes he's being judged by the company he keeps between his thighs and that he's supposed to have the expected rise in his Levis. Men who have experienced a lack of wind propping up their mainsails will tell you that the women they've been in bed with at such embarrassing moments weren't exactly thanking them for the experience.

Men are also aware that some twenty-first-century women keep ten-inch, three-speed, sure home-run hitters in the on-deck circles next to their beds in case their usual cleanup batters are in a slump. What a vote of confidence those feminine power tools provide mortal men. Any truly honest guy will hasten to tell you he doesn't want to compete with that towering, ribbed torpedo she keeps pristine and polished in its velvet case waiting at her beck and call.

Given the marvels of modern technology, the hip, sexually progressive hot chick of today needs only a fertile imagination and a fresh set of batteries to savor the flavor of the big O. And this only provides further edification for the theory. I couldn't help noticing as I perused the sex-toys catalog while doing my research for this book, that the limp, flaccid vibrators and dildos were conspicuously unavailable for purchase. Alas, they must be available only by special order.

Manufacturing Manhood in the New Millennium

Many guys out there, more than will admit it, may be intimidated because they feel their sexual potency is being challenged. They may be struggling to perform, specifically because the sexual tables have been turned. The media and marketing folks aren't helping either.

Men are constantly reminded of just how important it is to maintain their erections. Television commercials for Viagra and Cialis are strategically placed during sports telecasts such as NFL and NBA games or PGA golf tournaments, to assure the targeted audience gets the message. Immediately after Tiger Woods skillfully employs his putter to sink his ball into the hole, the telecast cuts to a scene of a middle-aged couple furtively eyeing each other from their chaise lounges on the beach. They proudly profess satisfaction with such a great product and assure confidence that all will be upstanding as usual in the bedroom.

Even during the morning news programs, the observant guy can catch a commercial for one of these surefire cures for ED (erectile dysfunction) while he trims his sideburns. One disclaimer given for the only-by-prescription variety is to call your doctor if your erection lasts for more than four hours. Four hours? If a man had an erection for four hours, he wouldn't call his doctor; he'd catch the first flight to the Playboy Mansion!

And the recurring message isn't restricted to television. In addition to print ads, newspaper ads, and radio spots, every male in America over eighteen with an e-mail address receives five to ten ads every day for magic potions, all organic of course, guaranteed to please their women by increasing their staying power and adding inches to their length. Never before have men been so constantly reminded of just how important it is to have an erection.

The Little Engine That Could—Not!

Women don't have the same element of pressure to perform as men do because they need only be ready to receive, to host the incoming source of pleasure—figuratively speaking, to open the tunnel so the train can come in. But the men are sporting the train, ceaselessly subjected to the constant vigilance of a scrutinizing conductor, so they feel pressured to fuel up and power their locomotive straight ahead.

Tom, fifty-one, a telecom sales rep from San Diego, California, says he's felt this way more than once. "When I'm with a woman, I feel like she's constantly checking me out to see if I'm hard. I don't remember ever worrying about that when I was in my twenties, even my thirties. But now, it can really be scary. Unless I take a Viagra first, and it always gives me a splitting headache when I do, I spend half my time laying on my stomach so she can't tell!"

A lot of men feel they are more vulnerable to suffering from performance anxiety because they are being judged in no small part by whether they're getting it up quickly enough and keeping it up long enough to successfully complete the job. If for any reason a man isn't fully "ready," a woman can see it, she can feel it, she can question it, even criticize it. She can complain about it, wonder about it, and worry that she may somehow be the cause of it. She can even be somewhat sympathetic toward it. But the fact still remains: he is the one with the obvious problem on public, or should I say *pubic,* display.

Like the main character from the famous children's story, *The Little Engine That Could,* a man may commit himself to silently affirm, "I think I can, I think I can, I think I can," only to have Mr. Wiggly shout back at a deafening decibel, "Oh no you can't, Oh no YOU CAN'T, OH NO YOU CAN'T!" Men want women to understand just how sensitive an issue this can be.

Gary, fifty-seven, a consultant from Frisco, Texas, says he's one of them. "Nothing is more embarrassing than when, try as I may, I just can't make it happen and I know she knows it too. One woman I was with asked me if it was her. Of course I said it wasn't, but I wondered how that must have made her feel. And that made me feel even worse."

Dan, a sixty-year-old retired business executive from Scottsdale, Arizona, says he just wants women to be understanding. "I do use Viagra, been using it for two years, and I love it. But there are still some times when I've been out of it, or it hasn't quite kicked in yet, that I struggle. The kind of woman I want to be with is the one that tells me it's okay and that we can just do other things that feel good. At my age, I just can't hit a home run every time."

Secret No. 3 that men think but don't tell women is, *"Don't test for the erection!"* As we said earlier, every man knows he's being judged at least in part by what's going on between his legs. And this is a particularly sensitive area for men over forty. It's challenging enough for guys that they've already peaked sexually by around eighteen and that women don't hit their sexual summit until well into their thirties and beyond. The last thing a man needs is to have a woman hunting around down there before he's ready, only to find that his bird has indeed flown south, or worse, hasn't even made it up north just yet.

Bob, forty-five, a financial planner from Taos, New Mexico, was bold enough to speak up about this one. "I absolutely hate it when a woman starts checking me out to see if I'm hard yet. I don't remember even thinking about that when I was in my twenties, but I'm forty-five, and let's just say that guy down there doesn't always play along like he used to. He has his days, but he has his off days too, and sometimes it takes a little longer for me to get ready. I like a woman who will sort of steer clear until I give her the green light."

A guy can be intimidated by a woman pushing, plowing her way into his pants, attacking and advancing faster than a drug addict in a rehab clinic after a pack of Camels. She's launched a sexual salvo across the bow and scored a direct hit into his psyche, and he hasn't even manned his torpedo yet. The more savvied and skilled ladies who know Secret No. 3 perform subtle but effective recon by employing the hugging maneuver or the forearm brush. They wait to execute the direct smash-and-grab technique until they receive the prompt to proceed.

Still, most men do not like to be tested. And contrary to the opinion of some, doing push-ups and yelling, "Go marine raiders!" doesn't help. Thankfully, these days the little blue pill and its teammates are suited up and ready to come off of the bench as needed, but the point is that guys would prefer for women to be pleasantly surprised when they discover just how much of a turn-on they are rather than trying to solicit confirmation prematurely.

Since the erection is unique to men, they should have the right to control access to it. Women have long argued that they should have the right to control who has access to their bodies, and should they become pregnant, the right to make the choice regarding whether to carry their fetuses to full term. Guys should likewise be in control of who has access to their bodies, and since only they can suffer the humility and embarrassment of the unsightly LPS (limp penis syndrome), it makes perfect sense they should be given the right of first refusal regarding its point-in-time utilitarian bend.

Comedian Robin Williams said it best when he offered, "God gave men two heads, but only enough blood to operate one of them at a time." Aggressively pouncing on head No. 2 while forging forward in surprise attack mode can cause the limited blood supply of the male humanoid to flood into head No. 1 at warp speed.

Thrusting headlong into assessing the quality and state of the erection may be forcing an improvisational response many men are simply not prepared to provide. Head No. 1, at least theoretically the thinking head, is still trying to assimilate the concept of male laser hair removal, facials, manicures, and the fact that Matthew McConaughey keeps waxing his chest. It may be a while before Head No. 2 can accept a visitor snooping around down there well ahead of her scheduled arrival time.

Men want to be gallant heroes to women. And even though they have their flaws, they'd rather have more control over which ones get exposed. No one ever knew if Superman had a problem "down there" because the focus was on his vulnerability to kryptonite. Likewise, most guys are okay with women exploring the tattoos on their butts, the birthmarks on their inner thighs or the thinning spots on their heads. But they really wish women would have the decency to sidestep the sacred area of their demilitarized zones until their troops are at attention and ready to engage!

6

HASTE MAKES CHASTE

Secret No. 4: "Don't jump our bones before we're ready."

Most guys still want to be the quarterback when it's game time in the boudoir and are thrown for a loss each time their wide receiver starts calling the plays. In response, women who take advantage of this secret modify their strategies just a bit to give men a little more time to adjust. They aren't so quick to the dance and play a little of the lady-in-waiting game. Guys want to feel like the big men on campus and respond well if shown a little deference. Smart women know that the first thing they should stroke on men is their ego.

Sex and the City

Perhaps nothing has advanced the cause more for women feeling a new sense of empowerment in their approach to enjoying sex than the fictional HBO original series *Sex and the City*. Some have even referred to the show and its big-sister feature film as representing a milestone for American women. Allegedly, millions of female viewers, even teenagers, have adopted the same predatory approach to "scoring" they see so often portrayed in the shows. Various newspaper and magazine articles, television news features, and other social commentary have even suggested there may be a correlation between the way of life depicted on the show and the actual behavior of young women in real-world America today.

SATC features four single women in New York City who endeavor to have it all, their self-ascribed success often being defined by the company they keep in bed. The central characters of the show are attractive, hip, oversexed, mid-thirties and fortyish femes sole who have twisted the old adage, "Politics makes for strange bedfellows." Here, Samantha, Carrie, Charlotte, and Miranda are in a never-ending quest for strange fellows to bed.

To call them predatory would be an understatement, like suggesting that Angelina Jolie *might* have had collagen treatments on her lips. Apparently, a significant percentage of females, even those barely eligible for pubescent status, and especially those in the mainstream party circuit across America, are attempting to imitate the behavior of these fictional characters and leverage it to their benefit.

So what's the problem? Wouldn't most guys be dancing in the streets over this kind of news? Ordering ribbed Trojans by the case? Stocking up on Viagra? Salivating to exploit the benefits of what could arguably be called the greatest dating milestone since the invention of crotchless panties? Okay, maybe, but let us not forget one very important fact: new age "ladies" are doing all of this in the one area guys thought would remain their exclusive territory, even *after* the feminist movement.

Secret No. 4 that men think but don't tell women is, *"Don't jump our bones before we're ready."* No fine wine should be served before its time. Remember the plug and the wall socket. Poor execution could create a case of haste makes chaste.

Jim, fifty-two, a painter from Madison, Wisconsin, offers this piece of advice. "I can remember when I was in college and just couldn't get enough sex. I wanted it every day. But at my age now, I just can't perform like I used to, and honestly, I don't really have the drive I used to either. If I make love once a week, I'm happy. But my advice to women is to take it slow when they're with a man. Don't rush us because it can make us feel intimidated, like we have to perform on command. And especially as we get older, that's just not as easy to do as it once was. So, take your time, and let it all happen as it will. Otherwise, we might quit early and catch a game on ESPN."

Tom asks, "Why don't women let us feel like the men they wish we would be? We may never actually be the Johnny Depp or Brad Pitt they secretly desire, but we could get a hell of a lot closer to it if we think they view us as their personal, special stud muffins."

Dan wonders why women don't allow men to take the lead, at least in the very beginning. "Why can't they let us be more like traditional guys for a bit, just for a little while? Let us be the directors in our own little fantasy flicks."

Gary agrees. "Yeah, I wish they'd let us take the lead for the first dance or two. After that, they can be the captain, fulfill their wildest fantasies. I'd be fine with that."

Guys can change. But look at it rationally. Guys don't change their underwear until it fails the sniff test, usually after about the fifth consecutive day. Is it realistic to expect they can change their sexual anticipatory schemata overnight? Expecting them to change the way they play the boy-meets-girl, boy-asks-girl-out, boy-initiates-sex-when-boy-is-ready game with one wave of a magic wand is a tall order.

Men are always taking the rap for being unfeeling, unemotional, and focused only on themselves. Come on, is that really fair? Just look at the evidence. They feel really bad when their favorite team loses, get real emotional about hair loss, and are flawlessly focused when in command of the remote control. Remember, we're talking about *guys* here.

Deep down men really want women to let them be men. Dan brings that focus back to sex specifically. "This may sound funny, but when it comes to sex, if just in the very beginning, women could let us at least think we're in charge, let us lead in the bedroom the first time or two, they'd see that we would come around, and after that they could likely take the lead just as much, if not more, than we do."

Women might think of it being much like training a puppy. It's messy at first, you've got to praise them for even the simplest successes, and they have to learn to hold it and wait until the appropriate time to let it out. But once they're fully housebroken, oh, what a true joy they are to have around.

Though *Sex and the City* is a funny, entertaining, and enlightening show and one of my personal favorites—it may be best if we don't idolize four sexually starved single women who live a delusional lifestyle, convinced they've got the world by the tail. Accepting Samantha, Carrie, Charlotte, and Miranda as role models makes about as much sense as believing Siegfried and Roy are just good friends.

These *Sex and the City* characters are fictitious figments of writers' imaginations (albeit fertile ones), and though I grant you such behavior does in fact happen in real life, it is the exception rather than the rule. Not all women are so demonstrative in making fun of men, taking advantage of men, or exploiting men for purely sexual purposes.

Women who capitalize on this secret know that when it comes to sex, if they're too hasty and aggressive, they may get turned down. If women want to assume the traditional male role, they need to be willing to accept what men have been living with for years. It is a numbers game, where no is heard far more often than yes. And just as women have been spouting for years, no means NO!

On the other hand, there are approximately forty million singles older than forty in the United States. Assuming roughly half of them are men, it means there are twenty million guys out there who are over forty, single, alone, and horny. And that's just among the baby boomers. Including men in their twenties and thirties adds millions more, so the market for prurient desires is rather sizable, and the numbers could work in favor of the more precocious women.

Still, uncovering secret No. 4 helps women remember that coupling aggressive behavior with the fragile male ego can set the stage for a series of pretty memorable, if not infamous, evenings. Women in the know make their choices with discretion. They also know that when they enter the two-hundred-meter freestyle of sex there is no lifeguard on duty.

By contrast, men need to wake up and get into the twenty-first century. It's okay for women to initiate sex. It doesn't portend certain castration for guys, and it doesn't emasculate them in any way. They should enjoy it! And if they're not in the mood at the particular moment the women are, they can just say, "Not now, honey, I have a headache."

Guys need to be smart, careful, and judicious when picking a sexual partner. Not all women are releasing their feminine pheromones into the vaporous confines of men's personal spaces like strategically placed pins in a voodoo doll. Choose wisely and by all means, have fun!

Note to guys: adapt to the blowing winds of change where you can, and just say no where you can't. Note to girls: Help your men out. Understand how they've been prewired and be patient with them. Otherwise, you won't get their best efforts, their *full* attention, because they'll be too busy worrying about how they measure up to all the rest or whether Mr. Wiggly will be up for the task. And I think we can all agree, 'tis better to have the problem licked from the start, to have it well at hand, than to have to pack it up and send it home because it failed to fire on command.

7

It's Helga from Helsinki!

Secret No. 5: "Act more feminine, and we'll be more masculine."

"Me Tarzan . . . you Jane. Me wear loin cloth from Abercrombie & Fitch . . . you wear thong and push-up bra from Victoria's Secret. Me Man . . . you woman. . . . Me fix car . . . you fix Tarzan macaroni and cheese, with extra cheddar.

For generations men were expected to be masculine and women feminine. Lisa Douglas from the old TV show *Green Acres* wasn't exactly the perfect prototype, but when compared to Ralph, the Douglases' tomboy carpenter, she was the Madonna. In the good old days men were men and women were women, and there were no unisex bathrooms!

Mrs. Douglas may have been replaced by the more resourceful, self-sufficient, and resilient Bree Van de Camp Hodge or Lynette Scavo from *Desperate Housewives*, but what all three of these women share in common is that at the end of the day, it's their femininity more than anything else that attracts both their TV husbands and the show's viewers. What we don't see them do is aggressively abandon that femininity in their sexual relationships.

Since men have historically taken the lead in the bedroom, for many of them, a change in that established protocol creates an antithetical defining of what is masculine and feminine. Men tend to define their virility relative to women's femininity. Just as there is no in without an out, no up without a down, no push without a pull, some men individuate themselves as "masculine" based specifically on "feminine" being its opposite.

When women come across as too masculine, it turns most guys off. Tarzan was Tarzan in large part because Jane was Jane. Victoria's real covert secret is the selling of overt femininity. For most men, sexually aggressive women are simply not feminine. Men want to be Tarzan, lose the loin cloth, and push off the push-up en route to the treasure trove that lies beneath Jane's thong. When they encounter Helga from Helsinki charging relentlessly at their Netherlands, they tend to call a time-out for a much needed ice breaker first.

In fact, a lot of men have begun insisting they get to know their prospective partners a little better first, and they're saying no for many reasons. Examples include, "She's too fast, I can't trust her; she could have some STD, or be carrying HIV!" Or, "If she's this fast with me, how many other guys has she done this with?" Some have even said, "Hey man, I don't want to be just another notch on her headboard!"

Wow! That's an original one. It has always been the *guys* who have been accused of exploiting the one-night stand. The girls have complained that they don't want to be just another piece of meat, his next conquest, or the next notch on *his* headboard. What's with this sudden one-eighty? Has the hunter in fact become the hunted? Has the thrill of the chase been extinguished for guys because they're now the ones being chased?

Secret No. 5 that men think but don't tell women is, *"Act more feminine, and we'll be more masculine."* Henry, a forty-nine-year-old high school teacher from East Moline, Illinois, has a very specific message for women. "I'll be the first to say I'm into the way a woman looks just as much as the next guy. But what I really want women to know is that, no matter how good they might look, if they want a guy to be masculine, you know, be a man's man, then they need to act feminine, not just look it."

Joseph, thirty-seven, a financial consultant from Seattle, Washington, agrees. "If a woman dresses attractively, is ladylike and pretty, but doesn't act feminine, I'm okay with that, but I'll treat her as just one of the guys. And if she acts like one of my competitors at work or at the gym, for example, I'll simply reciprocate and treat her the same way but choose someone else to date or pursue romantically."

Most men have trouble acting like men when the women in front of them come across as more masculine than they are. Guys are naïve. They still think men are supposed to be tougher than women. They actually believe that men wear Brut cologne and Axe deodorant and women wear Beautiful and Dove. Men want women to be feminine, not feminists. Guys still want to hear, "You had me at hello."

In a guy's mind, being feminine doesn't discount a woman's strength and abilities, but instead is alluring and entices him to accept and celebrate both. I'm reminded of that cliché, something about catching more flies with honey than with vinegar. Women have the ultimate arsenal at their beck and call. All they have to do is choose to use it. Smart women who capitalize on Secret No. 5 know the number one way to snag a masculine man is by baiting him with feminine charm.

Without femininity, there would be no masculinity. There would be no James Bond without the Bond girls, and Rhett Butler just wouldn't be the same man if there were no Scarlett O'Hara. Worst of all, without his love interest Nell, Dudley Do-Right would likely be Dudley Do-Wrong!

Femininity is as femininity does. Apparently the game really has changed. After all, we do have those unisex bathrooms. Anybody want to invest in a new unisex thong shop? We could put one on every corner and call them Starbutts!

WORK

"My first order of business as the new CEO . . . scented company letterhead."

8

Man the Torpedoes...
the Patriarchy Is in Trouble!

Secret No. 6: "Women shouldn't be in charge at the office!"

Dave, thirty-six, a software salesman from Austin, Texas, is not a happy camper. He just found out that his favorite boss of the last five years is being replaced by someone named Cindy, and he is not too keen on the idea of having to report to a woman.

"A buddy of mine, we both sell software for the same company, was in a panic and waiting for me when I got to the office yesterday because he'd just found out that our boss had been transferred and the new boss coming in from another market to take his place is a woman. A WOMAN? Oh my God, our new boss is a woman? What's up with that? We're supposed to take orders from a woman now? I already do that at home! Well, I guess this means we can kiss the Friday-afternoon strategic planning 'luncheons' at the Sultry Fox Hole goodbye!"

I had no idea so much business was being conducted at strip joints. I thought guys went to watch dancers with names like Bambi and Dakota only *after* they took care of the business deal on the golf course first, the great American work ethic personified. Obviously some men still believe that while women can be valued and productive in the workplace, they should not be in charge, or at least, not in charge of *the men!*

For guys like Dave and his co-worker, having a woman for a boss can be as mortifying as tapping the shoulder of that platinum-blonde babe at the office Christmas party, only to see her turn around and introduce himself as Allan from accounting! They may need to cash in their frequent flyer miles for a one-way ticket into the twenty-first century. Women are capable of mastering a lot more than sliding up and down poles at their favorite R-rated watering holes.

Dave is one of those old-school guys who believes putting women in charge is fine when it comes to planning a special dessert for the church social, doing birthday-present shopping for the kids, or sending out thank-you notes. But putting them one-up to a man in the workplace is a sacrilege. When I interviewed him, he actually said, "Come on, man, can we be any more emasculated? This is bad, very bad. It's the pussy-fication of America! What's next, a woman president?"

For the millions of squires who were brought up to believe that the workplace is supposed to be a man's world, such an orientation should come as no surprise. Though many of these guys were in their late teens and early twenties when the feminist movement enjoyed its most vocal presence, most still tend to prefer a more traditional model where men are in charge and women work in supportive positions.

But Dave isn't one of those sexist, male-chauvinist pigs left over from decades ago, is he? He's only thirty-six years old, a Gen-X, New Age guy. Isn't he supposed to be a member of the more liberated male species? Why is *he* saying such misogynistic things? Could he be a baby boomer trapped in a Gen-X body? Maybe he's been spending too much time at the Sultry Fox Hole with his late-forties-something boss.

Or is there a deeper significance to all of this? Could it be that his apparent opposition to having a female rank above him at work is really masking some sensitive psychological issue that, once brought to his awareness, could be resolved? Why is he so uptight about having a woman for a boss? He would do well to take a closer look at the concept of being the boss.

The Boss

By traditional definition, a boss is the person in charge. The boss determines who does what, when, how, and with and for whom. A boss can control a subordinate's time and work load, even earnings. A boss is also the person who must comply with the two "never" rules. Rule one: Never forget to give a gift to your assistant on Administrative Professionals' Day. And Rule two: Never expect to *get* a gift from that same assistant on National Boss's Day.

An effective boss can teach, inspire, motivate, lead, and mentor. A particularly good boss can positively drive performance and facilitate powerful results. Conversely, a boss can also be intimidating, unyielding, hypercritical, unfair, and even offensive. A particularly bad boss can even debilitate subordinates, stressing them to the point of futility or fear, often resulting in termination or resignation of their employees. And a *really* bad boss hands out dart boards with their picture in the bull's-eye.

Forty years ago a *female* boss was virtually unheard of in the United States. And even today among the Fortune 500 corporations, barely 2 percent of the CEOs are women. Though it makes sense that seniority among well-entrenched, long-tenured men promoted from within may contribute to this negligible statistic, many women who aspire to leadership positions find that "getting upstairs" is still a formidable challenge in their corporate lives.

Interestingly, a significant percentage of women are voluntarily walking away from their corporate jobs to raise families or start their own home-based businesses. So some men may be landing top positions by default, as otherwise eligible female candidates bow out of contention.

Still, growing numbers of women are taking leadership positions in organizations throughout the country. In fact, 52 percent of middle managers are now women. Wait a minute. What was that? Fifty-two percent of middle managers are now women? But that's the majority! Shouldn't corporate America be making proactive efforts to achieve parity there, too? I haven't heard a single woman complain that there are not enough men at that level. They certainly complained when it was the other way around. Must be a simple oversight.

One particular woman received significant media play on her quest to become the boss, and Dave wanted to be sure I knew about it. He brought it to my attention because he was incensed over what he'd seen on a cable TV channel a few nights earlier. A sports-talk television program featured a story about one woman, we'll call her Joanne, who filed suit against a high school because she thought she was being unfairly denied an opportunity to be the head coach, to be the boss, for the *boys'* varsity basketball team. Dave had no problem with her being a coach, even the head coach, but he was adamant in his belief that she should coach the *girls'* team, not the boys'.

"I'm so damn tired of seeing these butch women trying to horn in on our world!" he complained. "Just look at sports on TV! You've got women reporters on the sidelines of NFL games and women doing commentaries on the court at NBA games. Yeah, like that chick Pam Oliver, whatever her name is, really should be standing next to Tim Duncan asking him what his strategy will be in the second half. NOT! Hell, in the NBA, even a couple of the *refs* are women! Women go into the locker rooms and interview the players too! It's all getting so ridiculous. It's gone way too far! Why can't women do the women's sports and men do the men's? But this high school coach bit *really* pisses me off! No woman should be coaching a boys' high school basketball team, period, end of sentence."

At first I suggested Dave take a sedative and try to relax. But wait a second. Might he have a valid point? In high school sports, a coach is much like a boss. Truth be told, a coach is a boss, controlling every moment of time and activity of every player under his or her charge. Should a woman really be in charge of a group of adolescent boys?

High school sports are typically managed as a collective dictatorship, where the athletic director, almost without exception a male, and often also the head football coach, is a figurative god. He rules over his forces, occasionally descending from the mountaintop to issue a policy change or pat some macho tough kid on the ass for flattening the opponent from a rival school the day before. The AD's direct subordinates are the coaches, typically former athletes themselves, who in turn have dominion over the players.

Within such a unilaterally designed hierarchy, far too many coaches follow the lead of their ADs, and run their programs in Draconian style. Such a model can be seen no more clearly than on the high school football field. In thousands of towns across America, secondary-school academics take a second seat to the myth and magic of life on the gridiron. Time spent in athletics is often more than triple the time spent in academics, and daily practices extend long past sundown, ending only when and how the coach mandates.

And football isn't the only sport where strength, stamina, and athletic prowess separate the interscholastic Herculean haves from the have-nots. Even the basketball coaches tend to be the macho, "Drop down and give me fifty!" dictators of athletic enterprise. They expose the weak, accentuate the strong, and tend to remember the first names of only those players tough enough and good enough to make the starting five. So *is* the head coaching position for a *boys'* high school basketball team really the right job for a woman?

For some strange reason, perhaps known only to Joanne herself, she wanted in this fraternity of male jockocracy. More important, she wanted her subordinates to be male too! Could she be harboring a long-standing "Men are pigs!" attitude left over from the original bra-burning days and just want to dominate the enemy? Or might she just like young boys? It most certainly can't be because she thinks the boys are superior to the girls as players. Can it?

For whatever reason, it wasn't acceptable in Joanne's mind for her to coach the girls' team. Neither was it a situation where there were no men, or only less-qualified men, available for the job. In fact, there were *several* men wanting the same job, with equal or better qualifications. She simply wanted to coach the boys and was prepared to pursue whatever legal action necessary to secure the job. Here's the rub: Joanne sued the school and the school district, and when all was said and done, SHE WON! Thus a woman became the head coach of a high school *boys'* basketball team.

But is it wise to have a woman in a high school *boys'* locker room? Face it, a woman interacting with a group of young striplings, some of whom haven't even experienced the dropping of their scrotal sacks yet, can be deleterious to the youngsters' developing psyches. Some of those kids don't even have *hair* down there yet! Let's at least give the players a chance to successfully complete the transition through puberty before Alice from *The Brady Bunch* reprimands them for not using Tinactin to cure their jock itch.

In high school locker rooms, it can be embarrassing enough just trying to fit in as one of the guys, without compounding the issue by adding the presence of a woman. Fifteen- to eighteen-year-old boys don't even want their *mothers* to see them naked, much less Miss Ballbreaker from Girl's PE. For Dave, this particular form of woman-on-top gig is taking on a whole new meaning, and trying to make sense of it all has his mind scrambling faster than a Baghdad taxi driver leaving the airport.

Secret No. 6 that men think but don't tell women is, *"Women shouldn't be in charge at the office!"* Call it patriarchal, call it chauvinistic, but a lot of men see no reason to change what has been working successfully for generations. There are roles some men believe are meant to be filled by women, and others are better fit for men. In many a man's mind, being the boss is a man's job. Ginger and Marianne may have been the hotties on Gilligan's island, but the skipper was the captain.

Tony, fifty-three, an executive with a national wireless company is definitely in that camp. "I have no problem with women working, and I am happy to have them working for me. But I just don't believe women should run companies. They tend to invest too much emotion and not enough logic into their work. I know I shouldn't be saying this, but I'm telling you what I really think. I just question why women should be in charge."

Dave is quick to agree with Tony. "Men are meant to be leaders. You can't get emotional when you're in charge. Can you imagine what it would be like if a woman was a general on the battlefield? I'm not meaning to offend women, I'm really not. I just think there are some things women are better at than men and some things men are better at than women."

Tony, Dave, and Dave's co-worker probably question why women should be allowed to sit in the driver's seat in the car, too. They seem to have a problem with women in authority, and they have obvious issues with women running companies. Seems like a clear-cut case of penis-in-charge envy to me.

Absurdity notwithstanding, this is a secret that more men think but don't say than most women might imagine. But why would this be a problem for men? In Dave's case, other than missing those meetings at the strip joint, and even his new boss could endorse that if she were so inclined, why would his work life have to be any different simply because his boss is a woman?

We need women to be in charge, too. Someone has to be able to organize the annual company picnic, and we all know we can't count on the guys to do that. Honestly, how much of a difference can there really be in the genders when it comes to managing a business? Does the sex of the boss really matter that much? Women who understand and capitalize on this secret know Dave and his buddies just need to work it out in therapy. The last time I checked, there were two distinct executive washrooms, one with urinals and one without.

9

THE HONEY-DO PARADIGM SHIFT

Secret No. 7: "We already have a woman for a boss at home."

For thousands of men across the country like Dave and his co-workers, high school sports programs and the coaching of them notwithstanding, the reality of more and more women assuming leadership roles in the world of work may be the pill that's just a bit too big to swallow. They wonder how the guy with a woman for a boss feels when he has to come home after a day of order-taking from a person he perceives as some feminist, corporate-ladder-climbing superwoman, only to take another set of orders from the ultimate boss, his wife?

Isn't one woman-boss enough? How much humility is a man supposed to suffer? Multiple women telling guys what to do could really mess with their heads. If they're called *Honey-Do's* at home, would that make them *You'd-Better-Do's* at work?

Gordon, forty-nine, a veteran IT manager from Hartford, Connecticut, says he's really having a hard time remembering what it was like to be a real man. "I can remember ten years ago before I got married, I was in charge of myself, my home, and at work I was a supervisor, and my boss was a guy. I felt like a man at home and at work. But now, after ten years of marriage, my wife runs the house and constantly gives me to-do lists. I mean actual written lists of stuff she wants me to do! Then, when I go to work, my boss is a woman there too. Sometimes I really feel like I'm all alone as a guy, like I need some other guys around to help me remember what it's like to be a man. I feel like I'm constantly catering to women and worse, that they're watching my every move."

Freud Has His Hands in Here, Too?

Interestingly, there may be psychological precedent for the angst both Dave and Gordon are suffering. Psychoanalytic theory suggests that infant boys, seeing that they are physically different from their mothers, need to learn to separate from them and become more like the humanoid to which they look most similar, which is of course, typically their fathers. That might not be true for the kid lying in his crib looking up at Marilyn Manson, but it certainly is for most little boys.

The actual term used to describe this dynamic is *individuation*, and to individuate means to detach from the mother and develop an autonomous sense of self, to become one's own individual. Since the boy is not female and thus is not like his mother, he individuates away from the model of "female" and toward the model of "male," like his father.

In the typical family model of forty years ago, boys tossed the football with Dad, worked in the garage with Dad, watched sports on TV with Dad, hunted and fished with Dad, and generally developed a male bond with Dad. Girls cooked in the kitchen with Mom, did the laundry with Mom, went shopping with Mom, enlisted Mom's help with their dollhouses, and likewise developed a female bond with Mom.

Boys and girls also observed and understood that with rare exception, Dad was in charge at home, the ultimate boss as he sat at the head of the table and issued commands such as, "Eat everything on your plate." And if a child had misbehaved during the day, at home or at school, Mom would simply state, "Wait until your father gets home!" Dad was both judge and jury, and every kid knew it. Power was both implied and real.

Individuating boys also noticed that ministers, priests, and rabbis were men. Most if not all of their coaches were men, and in the military, they took orders from men. Men were the captains of business, religion, and politics too. Naturally, boys grew up believing that once they left the nest they would take orders from men, not from women.

Young guys entered the workforce having spent the first twenty-odd years of their lives oriented to accept clearly defined gender roles where, with the possible exception of school teachers, male authority was the accepted norm. This paradigm served as a socially prescribed support system of sorts for their efforts to individuate away from female control and toward male leadership instead.

Most men were accustomed to taking instructions from their mothers, and once married could respond to their wives in kind. But to answer to any other women seemed unnatural. Given this perspective, it makes sense that many guys find it hard to accept taking orders from any woman other than the one at home.

A lot of men growing up were taught that when they became adults, it would be their responsibility to secure good jobs, earn money, and provide comfortable lives for their wives and families. It was a common assumption they would work for men, not women, and that they would over the years earn a series of promotions that would one day lead to *them* being the boss. Their problem now may be less the belief that women aren't capable of being in charge, and more that they simply shouldn't be, even though such thinking has been proven meritless.

Having a man for a boss has been a long-standing cultural standard and what most guys have simply come to expect. Secret No. 7 that men think but don't tell women is, *"We already have a woman for a boss at home."* Jack, a fifty-one-year-old marketing executive from Newport Beach, California, is one such man. "I'm sorry, I know it's not politically correct to say this, but the truth is, I'm just not comfortable with the idea that I would report to a woman at work. I basically already do that at home. I report to my wife! I think if something changed at work and our VP/GM was replaced by a woman, I'd probably find another job. I guess it's my upbringing, but I just think men are supposed to be the leaders."

There is another reason why men might not want to report to women, something to do with eye candy. Evan, thirty-five, a retail store manager from Dana Point, California, thinks it's risky to report to a woman who is hot-looking, especially if she comes to work dressed seductively. He says it can put a man in a precarious position with his wife.

"It can be a real problem when the boss happens to be hot-looking and dresses provocatively. I mean, it's bad enough when one of my co-workers does it, but I don't report to her. But if my boss wears some low-cut outfit showing off her cleavage or a dress that's so short when she sits down and crosses her legs you can see clear up her thigh, it makes me very uncomfortable because my wife may see her as competition, and it makes it real hard to explain to her the reasons why I have to work late from time to time."

It's Part of My Personal Life, Too?

Women's assumption of leadership positions in the workplace has had an adverse affect on the dating lives of some men. Ron, fifty-two, an insurance agent from Omaha, Nebraska, says he's really having trouble and wishes he could find a more understanding woman.

"I was married for fifteen years and divorced about a year ago. I'll tell you, I really feel like a fish out of water. All the women I meet seem like they're on some power trip. They spend most of their time telling me how successful they are and how much money they make. I went out with a woman a couple of weeks ago, and she kept calling the folks who work for her 'my people.' It made me feel uncomfortable. I have twenty people that work under my leadership, and I never call them 'my people'. I just wish I could find a girl that I could connect with. Too many women are trying to impress me with their corporate success instead of just enjoying spending time together."

Many men also report feeling pistol-whipped at home, the by-product of being on the receiving end of what they perceive to be unending orders and injunctions from their wives. Some men admit they've adapted to it as an accepted, even expected form of domestic indentured servitude. In fact, when a survey of married couples celebrating their golden wedding anniversary was conducted, the men were asked the secret to the success of their marriages. The most often heard response was: "I learned forty-nine years ago to simply say 'Yes, Dear.'"

Although men may have accepted their lot at home, they're accustomed to using the good ole' boys club at work as their compensatory sanctuary. To many men, the only woman they may be willing to take orders from is the one they married, so answering to any female other than their wives is tantamount to taking a direct hit below the belt. It's simply not something they've been programmed to do, and they wonder what reaction they'll get from their wives when informed of the reality that another woman will be telling *their* honeys what to do!

Taking orders from the woman they've pledged to honor and obey for richer or poorer, in sickness and in health 'till death do them part, so help them God, comes with the territory. But to have such a subordinate relationship with another woman just doesn't seem right.

Could this be the beginning of a whole new form of marital infidelity? It could be a whole new means of cheating; a guy is found guilty of willingly taking orders from a woman other than his wife.

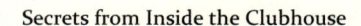

I can see the divorce papers now. The reason for dissolution of the marriage: irreconcilable orders and injunctions.

10

June Cleaver Has a Briefcase?

Secret No. 8: "Mothering doesn't work at the office."

Inquiring minds might wonder why women even *want* to be in charge at work. What about being the boss is so appealing? Do women want the position simply because the opportunity to have it has finally become a reality for them? Because they can finally fill the spots that were heretofore reserved almost exclusively for men? Why do so many women want figuratively to strap on the strap-on and smoke a stogie with the guys?

The overall perception is that the boss is the smartest, or at least most privileged, person in the room. The boss is also the one with the most decision-making power and is usually the highest paid. In some ways a boss is like a parent. The boss controls others, sets the agenda, and delivers the discipline too. Given that most women are relationally oriented caregivers and caretakers, being in charge at work may be a vocational manifestation of the homemaker role. But can mothering be listed as professional experience on a resume?

Whatever the reasons, more and more women are aspiring to be bosses, and many are ascending through the corporate ranks and earning their spots at the top. But what core competencies are needed to be a boss? Are they knowledge, integrity, and a unique skills set? Do parenting skills help one be an effective boss? How about brains—you know, intellect? Does one really need to be the smartest in the company to be the boss?

Maybe it really is more about mothering, running things in the workplace, much as they do around the house. A lot of men think that since women are highly experienced as managers at home, including overseeing their husbands and children, they naturally gravitate toward leadership positions at work. But guys don't want their *moms* showing up at work. Art, thirty-three, an ad agency sales rep from Denver, Colorado, says he wants only one mother.

"When I became an adult, I expected to live my own life, independent of my mother's rules. It's traditional for men to be in charge, and that's what I'm used to. I still have to answer to my mother, even at thirty-three! I think I can learn to accept reporting to a woman at work but not if she treats me like my mother does. Quite frankly, one mother is enough."

Secret No. 8 that men think but don't tell women is, *"Mothering doesn't work at the office."* Randall, thirty-nine, a human resources director from Lubbock, Texas, says he regularly sees women manage the men under their charge using too much of a maternal approach.

"I've had more than a few complaints from men that their boss, a woman, has treated them just like their mothers do. One guy said his boss calls him Tim until she is not satisfied with something he's doing, and then she calls him 'Timothy!' Another guy complained that when he was heading out to make a sales call, his boss reminded him of every item, one by one, that he must remember to cover at the meeting, and then told him not to forget his coat because it was cold outside."

When Randall told me this, I thought he was kidding. But then I remembered the research. As we've said before, women are wired to be nurturing caretakers. It really makes sense that they might behave as he described. As but one example, think of the men you know in executive positions who rely on their administrative assistants quite literally to take care of their every need at the office and in much of their personal lives. We seem to expect such behavior from women in support positions, even applaud it. Why should it surprise anybody that we might see some of that same behavior from women in leadership positions?

Women have more experience working for men than men have working for women. The majority of guys in the workplace today have never had a woman for a boss. Reporting to one is a new concept to many of them, and it will take some time for them to accept and adjust to the change. Most of them are still on a quest toward emancipation by way of individuation.

The workplace is not the home place. Smart women pick up on this secret and refrain from being too bossy at work. Men want women to leave the mothering behaviors at home where they best belong. Though both sexes will tend to act in ways expected of their respective genders, men want the work environment to be more filial. Given a choice, guys prefer a sibling rivalry over an Oedipal conflict every time.

While sex type is genetic, gender is learned. Men expect certain behaviors from women, and women expect certain behaviors from men. Each one confirms gender to the other. Women don't want guys waxing their underarms and shaving their legs, and guys don't want women *not* to. But maybe *that* can change too!

When at work, men just want women, especially if their bosses are women, to treat them like co-workers, not like children. They don't want to be reminded to brush their teeth and put on clean underwear before going out in public, and they don't want their name called as it appears on their driver's license. Although I will admit, "Bond, Little Johnny Bond," just doesn't have the same ring to it.

11

THE WORM HAS TURNED

Secret No. 9: "What if women are actually better than us?"

What reasons could men have for being so concerned about their bosses being women? Maybe guys perceive it as a threat to their manhood. After all, men are supposed to be in charge. Might they fear other guys will think of them as less manly if they have to report to a woman? Maybe it hearkens back to the days when boys were boys and they didn't let girls in the game. Could that be it? Whether as co-workers and, especially, as bosses, maybe men don't want to compete with women, let alone report to them.

Little Boys and Sandlot Games

Or might it run deeper than that? Maybe it's more about not wanting to be beaten! Take sandlot baseball as but one example. While letting a girl play was strictly taboo, if it meant the difference between being able to field a full team or forfeit, there were many times little Sally was allowed to slip on the glove, take her spot in right field, and bat ninth in the order. When a girl was permitted to play, albeit only as a necessary and last resort, it really wasn't that much of a problem, unless of course she somehow managed to *outplay* the boys!

Maybe it's really all about the humiliation, or potential threat of humiliation, that presents itself the moment the girl takes the field. If no girl is in the game, the possible embarrassment of being beaten by one is eliminated. A guy would rather lose to another guy by a margin of twenty than to a girl by only one. Nothing can emasculate a man faster than to have a woman beat him at something. It goes against everything he's been taught since he was a toddler.

In the seventies, when middle-aged Bobby Riggs lost to then-prominent women's tennis star Billie Jean King in their famous "battle of the sexes" match, some of his macho buddies probably hauled ass faster than a cocaine dealer at the local Policeman's Ball. Men everywhere made excuses for Riggs: He was old, he was way past his prime, and he was not in top condition. And though each of these claims may have been true, they weren't voiced so adamantly until *after* the match was over and Riggs had lost.

In 2003, when Annika Sörenstam played in the PGA Colonial golf tournament, men throughout the gallery could be heard saying they pitied the poor guys she drew as playing partners. Though it would be bad enough to be beaten by her no matter whom a player was paired with, it would be even more humiliating to have to walk the course with her all day and see her score displayed on the same placard as theirs, especially if her score was better.

Maybe this woman-for-a-boss thing is really about men feeling beaten in the business world, but specifically, by women! If a man's boss is a woman, she's in a one-up position to him. She's the coach, and she's got the power and authority to keep him on the bench. Maybe the same dynamic that was present when they were children on the sandlot is now being played out in the real world of the corporate cubicle or executive boardroom.

More importantly, maybe the boys want a girl to play only if they are certain she will be relegated to right field and bat ninth in the order. They don't want her batting ahead of them in the lineup, do they? But what if the girl is really good? What if, heaven forbid, she's actually better than the guys?

How Men Really Feel

Secret No. 9 that men think but don't tell women is, *"What if women are actually better than us?"* Curious to explore this challenging idea more deeply, I conducted a round-table discussion session in Dallas, Texas, with several professional men. All white-collar executives, the guys in this particular group cited gender-specific reasons why they were not totally in favor of women holding key leadership positions. They claim their rationale is purely logical and not based on either the ability or professional skills sets of women.

Don, a fifty-seven-year-old CEO of a midsized company, said that because a boss fills a more important, more critical role in the company, the organization may be made more vulnerable to inconsistencies should a woman be in charge and become pregnant. "Look, I don't want to come across as being discriminatory in any way, but a work team, much like an athletic team, needs a coach. If a woman has to miss two or three months of work while on maternity leave, the team will likely suffer."

Robert, sixty-one, the CFO of a Fortune 500 company, observed that some expectant mothers become less effective during the last three or four weeks prior to taking maternity leave, and totally ineffective while gone for twelve weeks following the birth of the child.

"I agree with Don. But I would add that it is very difficult for a lot of women to keep up the high-pressured pace that comes with being in charge during the last few weeks before they take maternity leave, and most of the women I've known who take the leave are gone for the full three months the law allows. I think it's a good thing that women can take time off, but in my opinion the company, or at least that particular woman's work team, is compromised for about four months, and a lot can happen in four months."

James, a forty-seven-year-old vice president of sales for an energy company, was much more succinct. "It's simple. A guy doesn't get pregnant, so a guy wouldn't miss twelve weeks of work if he were the boss! Let's be honest here, how good a boss can a woman be if she's not around to do her job? Maybe there's a reason only women can get pregnant and men can't!"

Okay, maybe Don's and Robert's points make some sense. Teams can suffer without leadership, and for a lot of women, the last few weeks of pregnancy can take a toll on job performance. But it is doubtful the Great Creator chose women as the gender of humanoid capable of becoming pregnant to keep them from dusting off their resumes and applying for a job at Microsoft.

Many women have continued to be effective at work until the day they left to have their babies, and then continued to work some from home while on maternity leave. In the workplace today, everything from e-mails and Word documents to Excel spreadsheets and streaming video can be accessed and responded to via wireless smart phones, laptops, and personal home computers. Women in leadership or other roles can continue to work effectively throughout the entirety of their lawful leave of absence.

By the way, the same thing can be said of men. The Family and Medical Leave Act affords men the same opportunity to take leaves of absence when their babies are born, so they can exercise the same privileges and continue to do their jobs in the same ways. Pregnancy and the actual delivering of a child don't exactly make for a vacation. Mothering is no walk in the park either, so women are certainly no strangers to the concept of hard work.

Both men and women can miss work for extended periods of time for any number of reasons such as poor health, leaves of absence, or protracted vacations. Gender shouldn't matter when it comes to being in charge. In all fairness to these guys' arguments, maybe it's more accurate to say that *any* boss in absentia for months at a time, regardless of their reasons or gender, may be rendered, even if only as a result of simply not being present, a less-than-effective one.

A couple of other men in the group suggested that women are too emotional to be put in positions of authority, that they're not good at keeping their cool under pressure. Carl, fifty-six, a sales manager at a brokerage firm, said his boss, a sales executive, is more of a driver than a leader. She's constantly on everyone in her charge, bitching at her subordinate managers for one reason or another, and is never satisfied with even their very best efforts. Yet when she became overwhelmed with an unusually heavy workload, she couldn't keep her emotions intact.

"This woman really lost it, I mean, freaked out! And it was over problems and issues that we managers deal with every day. But she broke down and cried in front of us during one of our weekly staff meetings, and frankly, it's not the first time it's happened. We all looked at each other and couldn't believe it, and it left several of us wondering if she is truly the right person for the job. She just can't keep her cool under pressure."

Bradley, forty-five, a controller for a manufacturing company, said he thinks women just lack managerial experience and are too nice. "In my opinion, women just haven't had the kind of experience most men have had at being the boss. Plus, the ones I've seen tend to be just the opposite of what Carl said; they are usually too nice and not tough enough."

But Dave tabled up yet another reason for not wanting a female boss. He enjoys those weekly "sales meetings" at the Sultry Fox Hole. The "boardroom," as he calls it, is a strip joint with a lavish lunch buffet and, according to Dave, an even more robust cornucopia of naked butts and boobs. He says he could give the woman-for-a-boss thing a try, but doesn't want to eighty-six the sojourns to see his girlfriends. Apparently it's something to do with the best sushi and crabmeat in town.

Dave obviously believes in mixing business with pleasure. He also used his time at the Sultry Fox Hole to "bond" with his boss. Now he's worried that his new boss Cindy won't understand or approve of his enjoyment of T&A being reported as a T&E expense.

Men don't want women to compromise their womanhood either. Fred, a sixty-one-year-old entrepreneur, says women don't need to try to be like men just because they're in charge. "I've seen women trying to act like men, cussing a blue streak, drinking heavily at business dinners, and even talking about sports with the guys at the office. I personally, and I know the same is true for several of my buddies, don't really want that. We like women to be women. It's fine if they have a drink with us or talk about sports if they're really interested, but we can tell when they're doing it just to try to get along with us."

The skills needed to be an exemplary boss aren't reserved exclusively for men. Maybe a woman boss isn't so bad after all. Think about it for a moment. Research shows that women are more relationally oriented than men, they're way better at details and follow-up, and have superior organizational skills. Their hearing is more acute, most have better verbal skills than men, and they are typically better at seeing things more globally or holistically. Plus, they can remember every single thing guys said to them a staggering six months or even six years ago! Most men can't remember what they had for breakfast.

Still, guys are not without their unique skills sets. Studies have shown that men have better mathematical abilities, higher aptitudes for mechanical applications, and ability to see things more linearly. They are also better at seeing patterns and abstract relations. Plus, history proves that men have been successfully fulfilling the "boss" role for thousands of years.

So, is one particular sex better fit to be the boss? Shockingly, the answer to such a question is probably no. Good bosses come wrapped in packages from both genders. Being a good boss has more to do with the work than with dresses or three-piece suits, although a male boss in a dress could make for an interesting staff meeting.

Microsoft's Excel, Word, and PowerPoint software programs are gender neutral. They all work the same whether a man or a woman uses them. A spreadsheet is a spreadsheet is a spreadsheet, two plus two still equals four, 97 percent of quota is still 97 percent of quota, and gross profit and return on investment are still gross profit and return on investment, whether the boss is male or female.

Bosses come in the form of leaders or drivers, authoritarian micromanagers or authoritative, permissive coaches or mentors. Some extend their subordinates freedom and autonomy, others don't. Whether those in charge are number crunchers or wine-and-diners—respected or hated by their subordinates—bosses can wear panties or boxers.

These guys disclosed a lot of reasons why they think men should continue to be in charge, some perhaps logical, others maybe more creative. What we haven't heard is anything about any pestering fear they may have about women being better than men. Maybe that's just one secret men can think but *never* say out loud.

12

Chivalry Is an Honor, Not an Order

Secret No. 10: "*ASK* us . . . don't tell us what to do."

Jim, fifty-seven, a business manager from Anchorage, Alaska, said it best. "We guys hate it when women tell us what to do. It reminds us of our mothers! I wish they would just *ask* us what to do instead. I'll do just about anything for a woman if she asks me, but my first reaction when I'm *told* what to do is to ignore it."

Most men genuinely want to be chivalrous. Men are prewired to want to provide and do things for women. Every guy grew up believing he should strip the shirt off his back and throw it over the puddle so the fair maiden could proceed safely ahead. Helping women is part of the male psyche. But a demand from a woman isn't the same thing as asking for help.

If a woman tells a man to step outside and fetch the newspaper, he'll press the remote and act like he didn't hear her. But if she *asks* him to please go get the paper, he'll drive to the nearest convenience store and return home moments later with the newspaper in one hand and a long-stemmed rose in the other.

Resourceful women can exploit Secret No. 10 that men think but don't tell women to their advantage. "ASK *us . . . don't tell us what to do.*" Guys really wish women would better understand this critical petition on their behalf. Men will go to the mat for women if they would simply ask for what they want rather than require or demand it.

Guys don't mind being coached or mentored by women when it's done by way of a suggestion or request. They just don't want assignments thrust upon them in the form of commands. And for the guys whose male role models were General Haig or the Godfather, it is especially hard to respond to orders from women. These guys perceive such injunctions as challenges to their expected gender roles as leaders.

A lot of guys think women are constantly trying to control them. But maybe women are attempting to establish only *expected* control. Since women have traditionally been expected to be the caretakers of the home and family, they may be just trying to do their jobs. It doesn't have to mean they seek to control a guy's every move, although some men report feeling such chokeholds.

While women attempt to be in control, men are expending equal effort to avoid *being* controlled. Men may act like boys sometimes, but they really don't want to be mothered. To many guys it feels more like they're being managed and modified, an M&M that doesn't taste very good and doesn't melt in their mouths either.

Men have historically been expected to be independent, to individuate and resist being controlled. Indeed, to be controlled, in the minds of a lot of guys, is to be seen as being less than manly. So some push-and-pull between the sexes is natural. The etiological roots go all the way back to the days of the hunters and gatherers.

Men bonded with other men, side by side, while out on the hunt, and women bonded with other women, face to face, while creating and sustaining the home and family. Men had to stay focused, keep their wits about them, be ever-vigilant, independent, self-sufficient and resourceful while on their quest for food. They had to learn not only how to survive, but how to be triumphant in conquest. They also had to do it in silence and stealth and be deadly accurate in attack lest they become the entrée de jour.

By contrast, women had to learn to work together with other women while gathering staples for the home, caring for the children, and becoming nurturing, benevolent members of the community. They had to be adept at interacting effectively with others to manage the village properly. As a result, women developed better verbal communications skills than men. They became good talkers, while men mastered quiet vigilance, and for both genders each skill was a functional requirement. Ahh, so that's why so many women today can talk the paint off of a '57 Chevy while simultaneously baking a casserole and checking their e-mails!

The '50s and '60s version of this primitive form of communal living typically called for the men to go out into the workplace and compete to earn the money (hunting) while the women stayed at home to care for the dwelling and raise the children (gathering). Ward Cleaver wore a suit and tie to the office, but only because if he showed up in a sweaty loin cloth he'd be sent to HR straight away.

Although such a design worked well in prehistoric times, and was pretty darn effective even as recently as the early 1970s, it's not without its contraindications today. For example, since men had to spend a lot of time side by side in silence with one another—where too much talking could be a liability—today they tend not to be as socially oriented as women. This cultural side effect can leave women feeling adrift at sea without mates in whom they can confide or with whom they can share their deepest thoughts, desires, and dreams.

One prescriptive fix seems to be "Girls' Night Out," providing women with both the venue and companionship to support the interpersonal social interaction they need. Shopping, extended lunches, and, of course, the telephone also collectively serve to help satisfy the girls' need for the face-to-face, true relational intimacy they often find missing with their men.

And since men have long been charged with the responsibility to provide and protect, they tend to be more overtly competitive than women. "Boys' Night Out" provides the opportunity to do what men do best: compare, compete, and complain.

They typically compare everything from their cars to their bars. They compete over even the most meaningless stuff—like when they actually make a bet with each other about how many traffic lights it takes to get from the house to the dry cleaners and then drag race each other to prove it. And they complain about, what else, women!

Still, there can be a great benefit for those women who make the effort to ask rather than demand from men. At the subconscious level, men want to please women. When a woman asks a man to do something for her, thousands of years of evolutionary psychology kick in, triggering the provider and protector signals in his brain, and he consciously makes the decision to respond. Men really do want to please women, yes, even *outside* of the bedroom. And contrary to some popular opinions, they don't want to drag women by the hair into their caves. At least not anymore; it tends to disrupt the cable signal.

Frankly, men feel more masculine when they provide something for women, especially when they are asked. Just as we considered the supposition women want to do their expected jobs, it's fair to assume men do too. Smart women know how to exploit this often misunderstood characteristic in men. It's that swim-the-widest-ocean, climb-the-highest-mountain, and step-in-front-of-a-speeding-bullet thing.

Guys don't feel this way about other men. So the fix on this one is simple. Women should enjoy it, indeed revel in it! What a welcome exchange for the mere behavior of *asking* rather than demanding. Best of all, women don't even have to do anything special; all they have to do is just be women. And that shouldn't be too much to ask, after all, they've been perfecting *that* for years!

So if a woman says, "Don't do that now . . . I'm *trying* to sleep!" Is it a request or a demand? Maybe it depends on one's perspective.

Money

"Excuse me, sir, but considering what you just spent for dinner... you might suggest that your date pay for the $500 bottle of wine she's guzzling."

13

JUST WHOSE MONEY IS THIS ANYWAY?

Secret No. 11: "Their money should be 'our' money too!"

I believe anything fun worth doing can be done by midnight, and if it's worth doing after midnight, it can be done at home. But late one evening, well past midnight, I was quietly enjoying a nightcap in the bar at the Waldorf in New York when my utopian peace and quiet was upended by cacophonous rants from a guy who looked like one of those corporate commando types from the accounting department. Straddling a bar stool, wearing khaki Dockers, a button-down Polo shirt, and Cole Haan leather-tasseled loafers with matching belt, the prepster was complaining to his buddy and to anyone else who might show even the slightest interest.

"I wanted to surprise my wife, so I bought her a fancy new cell phone; the very one she said she wanted. When I gave it to her, she hugged me and thanked me. But then she said, 'You didn't actually *pay* for this, did you?' Before I could even respond, she bitched back, 'If I had known *that*, I would have bought it myself, because I don't want *our* money being spent like that!' Hey, I was just trying to do something special for her! What does she mean by '*our* money' anyway? She works—isn't her money our money, too?"

His domestic protest caught my attention, so I introduced myself, told him about my book, and offered to buy him another round in exchange for a brief interview. He said his name was Kevin, and he was more than willing to oblige. "What is she saying?" he continued without missing a beat. "That her money is just for her, none of it is for us? But my money isn't just my money anymore, now it's *our* money instead? She never said that kind of stuff when we were dating! I could spend my money any way I wanted then. How did my money become our money the day we married, but her money remained only *her* money?"

His friend Tom nursed a single-malt scotch and joined in. "Hey man, I know exactly what he's talking about. Ever since the kids entered junior high, my wife started working, and I hear it all the time. She wants to budget the money I make, but conveniently leaves out the twenty bucks an hour she's earning. I mean, just whose money is this anyway? If hers is hers, mine ought to be mine, right?"

After listening to Kevin and Tom pontificate about the financial nuances of married life, I cleared the tab and retired to my room. As I deliberated the whole money-sharing concept, I realized that it was no different from many other topics negotiated between couples. Some reach agreement easily, while others can be as far apart as Donny Osmond and Amy Winehouse writing their wedding vows.

Women and men tend to jump on the "thinking logically" superhighway from two entirely different entrance ramps. To the typical guy, the route a woman takes to offer up a sound conclusion for even the simplest of conundrums often becomes a feeder lane into a labyrinth of mind-boggling one-ways and detours, leaving him more lost than the town drunk at a Southern Baptist happy hour.

The cognitive pathways of the feminine mind can lead a man on a safari into the deepest, darkest jungles of dissonance, danger zones requiring highly developed survival skills. Around every curve some form of selective inattention might disarm him and expose his intellectual private parts to the harsh elements of irrationality. Women, on the other hand, can't seem to understand why, once again, guys don't simply stop and ask for directions!

Women have intuitive and sensory superiority over men, while men are better at shapes and spatial ability. What this really means is that women have a sophisticated radar system housed in the extra set of eyes they have in the backs of their heads. This highly sensitive, visceral system extends throughout their entire bodies. They use it often to detect such things as which woman is wearing a brand-new haute couture frock to the company Christmas party, knowing she will return it for a full refund the following day.

Simply stated, Kevin's wife Christine is seeing the overall impact on the family budget, while he simply sees a cell phone. Her special gifts notwithstanding, she may need to be reminded that it is a new millennium. The very street where Wally and the Beaver hid from Eddie Haskell nearly fifty years ago is Wisteria Lane today, replete with desperate, albeit self-sufficient housewives. Since Christine works, earns money, and makes up one half of their family, her money should also be family or, better yet, "our" money.

If you're a guy reading this, you probably empathize with Kevin. If you're a woman, you just don't understand his confusion; it all makes perfect sense to you. And if you're like most women, no doubt you'll probably want to *talk* about it. Guys tend to get real nervous when women say those infamous seven words: "We really need to talk about this."

Most guys just don't have the cerebral bandwidth to participate in the kind of gender-banter women find so normal and natural. When a woman starts to talk, the guy starts groping for the doorway, ready to bolt at the first sign of daylight. She's now verbally engaged on some matter she deems important, while he's searching for a well-timed, "Yes, dear," "You're right, dear," or "*Absolutely*, dear!" and a quick exit.

By contrast, a guy likes to keep things simple. If it walks like a duck, talks like a duck, swims like a duck, and takes a dump like a duck, well, it damn sure must be a duck! It has to make obvious sense to a guy, quickly, and with no real element of subjectivity, or he loses interest. Face it, ladies, if it isn't about fantasy football or fixing cars, hunting or beer drinking in the bars, most guys check out from the let's-just-talk gig faster than a stripper at a tax audit.

In an effort to gain a better understanding of Kevin's situation, I contacted Christine by phone one afternoon. As we talked, she confirmed what Kevin had understood her to say. "I've worked hard for ten years. I've earned my money; it's my money, and I should be able to spend it on anything I want." She staunchly defended her right to have total control over the scratch in *her* wallet.

When I told her Kevin had said that she believed his money should be used for both of them, for their family, for the "our" money account, she confirmed that as well. "Yes," she stated with confidence, "I said that, and I believe it. It should be our money because Kevin earns more than I do."

He actually earns only about 21 percent more than she earns, so I pressed her on the issue. At this point she seemed a bit irritated. "Look," she said impatiently, "he's the man. His money is supposed to be for both of us. That's the way it's always been, and that's the way it should be!"

That's the way it's always been? That's the way it should be? Does this stream of logic represent the way most liberated women think? Maybe I missed an important memo. Forgive me if I approach this logically, but I was under the impression that women have been laboring for the past forty years to *change* the way things have always been. Apparently, the more things change, the more *some* things tend to stay the same.

If one assumes guys should pay for everything, Christine's reasoning makes sense. Were Kevin the sole earner, the lone breadwinner of the family, his money would indeed be "our" money since it would be the *only* money. But Christine earns money too. Kevin might want to drop a subtle hint her way, maybe whisper something really rich in Christine's ear, some innocuous yet cogent command like, "Show me the money, honey!"

When it comes to spending money in a dating or marital relationship, we don't seem to be nearly as progressive in changing our perceptions as we have been regarding other gender roles. In fact, when asked who should pay when on a date, focus group after focus group said men should still pay. And when asked why, those groups that were exclusively made up of women unanimously declared, "That's the way it's supposed to be."

But is it? Is that *really* the way it's supposed to be? Historically, since women didn't earn money, they didn't have any money to spend, and therefore men were expected to pay. It made logical sense and was clearly understood and accepted by both genders. But now that women earn their own money, it simply isn't egalitarian for them to expect men to continue to pay for everything they do together. Though guys may still pay most of the time, they want women to ante up some legal tender for the "our money" account from time to time as well.

Secret No. 11 that men think but don't tell women is, *"Their money should be 'our' money too!"* In a marriage or seriously committed relationship, it simply isn't fair, nor does it make logical sense, that women should be allowed to bank their money while men do all the spending. If both people are working and earning money, they should both contribute to the cause.

Mike, forty-six, a draftsman from Leewood, Kansas, thinks couples should share their resources. "My wife works too. She earns about half of what I earn, so I don't mind being the one who pays most of the time. But I like it when she steps up and pays for stuff sometimes, too. I just don't think it's fair that a woman should be able to work and keep all her money for herself. I look at our life as a partnership, and we should share *all* of its assets. All money earned, or a mutually agreed upon percentage of it, should be considered *our* money."

Kevin and Christine live in North Carolina. He is a well-paid sales executive at a Fortune 500 company, and she is the director of human resources for a local corporation in Charlotte. Both are college-degreed working professionals. They classify as a dual-career family. This is an important distinction because, by definition, a career position typically includes having a long-term capability of contributing economic benefit to the family.

That Christine stated she would have bought the cell phone for herself, with *her* money, appears to hold a double meaning. She apparently sought to exercise control over two sources of income simultaneously, her own and her husband's. Wow, talk about revising the gatherer role. She wants to control not only what she gathers but what he hunts too!

What would cause Christine to seek such control of the finances? Why would she so casually assume that the money she makes is hers to spend as she wishes, while all of Kevin's earnings are carefully allocated for the family, each proposed expense rigidly scrutinized? From where would this apparent sense of entitlement originate? A quick step back in time and a visit to the world of Igor, Egor, and Ogor may yield some answers.

14

PLATINUM CARDS AND WHITE TABLECLOTHS

Secret No. 12: "Women can fork over some scratch once in a while too."

There is a simple, almost elementary explanation as to why women so naturally and willingly tend to let men pay every time the waiter delivers the check. Much as with Pavlov's famous dog, it's a conditioned response.

It *Was* a Man's World

Thousands of years ago, Igor, Egor, and Ogor, the prehistoric versions of Moe, Larry, and Curly, set out before sunup with visions of brontosaurus baby-back ribs dancing in their heads. They encountered Brute the Bronto, who salivated at the sight of three weird, hairy dudes in loincloths running around wildly, waving clubs in the air, and it instantly became a case of survival of the fittest. The three cavemen wanted to win the battle because a) they were all hungry, b) they wanted to get laid that night since they knew a lot of sexual tension would build up while out on the hunt, and c) the Flintstones' Burger Barn drive-through was closed at that time of the morning.

The women stayed behind, raised the children, and tended to the chores needed to keep the cave in order. When the men returned to the village with their spoils, the women skinned the ribs, stuffed the head, and prepared the meals, while the men read the sports section of the *Prehistoric Sun-Times* and sat gazing at the fire. Sound familiar? Apparently, the more things change, the more some things indeed stay the same. A few millennia ago, dinner was freshly killed meat served in a cave; today it's Chinese take-out on granite counter tops or surf and turf for two, with a platinum card on a white tablecloth.

For centuries, men have been the breadwinners, and women, the wives and mothers, were relegated to subservient, albeit supportive, roles. Indeed, there was a time in our country when women couldn't own property, couldn't testify in court, and didn't have the right to obtain legal guardianship of their own children. In fact, it took a constitutional amendment, ratified in 1920, even to grant women the right to vote.

In this patriarchal society, each generation of boys and girls continued to practice established protocols as they followed in their parents' footsteps. Adolescent males aspired to become the breadwinners, the chief roosters in the hen house, and to establish their homes as their castles. Nubile young women set out to be the homemakers and mothers, willingly supportive of their husbands, always seeking mates who could be "good providers."

Fifty years ago, most women in the United States did not work outside the home. Of those who did, approximately 40 percent held jobs such as secretary, bookkeeper, elementary schoolteacher, typist, cashier, seamstress, nurse, household worker, or waitress. Many worked for the phone company as telephone operators.

Most of the jobs women filled required little to no formal education, and regardless of their employ, their work was considered necessary but mundane. They were accordingly paid at the low end of the earning continuum. And where some women were employed in jobs traditionally held by men, they were paid about 60 percent of what their male peers were paid for the same work. Since men were considered the primary providers, they were paid more money.

Women typically married in their late teens or early twenties and secured a job until their husbands finished college or trade school and found gainful employment. They would then quit working to become mothers and homemakers. Men were not only the primary breadwinners, for most of mainstream middle-America, they were the *only* breadwinners. Since women didn't earn money, they didn't have any to spend. Hence, the accepted, even expected, cultural convention that men paid for everything. It made sense at the time.

This cultural dynamic could be observed in dating behaviors long before a couple was married. Gender roles were clearly defined as early as junior high school. Girls didn't call boys; they waited to be called. Boys knew they would take the lead in calling the girls, asking them out on dates, and paying all expenses related to those dates. Both boys and girls, from an early age, understood the males had access to the money, so *they* spent the money. It was standard operating procedure that if you were a guy, you paid, and if you were a girl, it was paid for you. The protocol was based both on common logic and accepted gender-role assignment.

Whether a date at the local theater for a movie and some popcorn, a trip to Hawaii for the honeymoon, or the new house in which to raise the family, the guy coughed up the dough because *he* made the dough. His money really was *our* money back then, and how it was earned and managed had a direct impact on the economic ebb and flow of family life.

This prevailing socioeconomic culture was regularly depicted on television shows such as *The Adventures of Ozzie and Harriet*, *Leave It to Beaver*, and *Father Knows Best*. Ozzie Nelson, Ward Cleaver, and Jim Anderson went to work and earned the money while their wives Harriet, June, and Margaret stayed home and took care of the house and family. Roles were clearly defined, accepted, and understood by parents and children alike.

Today it's *The Osbournes*, *Gene Simmons Family Jewels*, and *Meet the Barkers*. Sharon Osbourne has made her own fortune managing Ozzie's career. Shannon Tweed, Simmons' twenty-three-year common law partner and mother of his two children, made plenty of cash as a Playboy Playmate of the Year and movie starlet. And Shannon Moakler, the better half of the Barkers, is a successful model, beauty queen, and television actress. All three dads earn money, and a lot of it, but all three moms rake in plenty of scratch too. And none of them stay home to take care of the house and family. Perish the thought they would do a job the housekeeper or nanny can do.

What Have You Done for Me Lately?

In 1963, the United States established the Equal Pay Act, a federal law prohibiting wage discrimination based on gender. Women entered colleges, universities, and the workforce in growing numbers and began making their own money. Still, a disparity between the potency of a man's financial resources and those of a woman continued to exist.

With rare exception, a woman could not get a car loan by herself. She typically couldn't secure a mortgage for a house alone, either. She had to have a man co-sign for the commitment. In fact, car loans and home mortgages were in *his* name, or at best, registered jointly, listing his name first. But some women figured out how to be both industrious and resourceful.

By the early seventies, the sexual revolution was in full swing. Prurient intrigue pushed puritanical beliefs to the back of the bus and opened the door to a new type of barter system. A woman could enjoy casual sex with a man and exchange her goods and services for his available resources. The right guy, possessing the requisite cash, could be inspired to pay off the balance of her credit card, take her on that sun, sea, and sand tropical island excursion, and provide her a regular staple of white-tablecloth dinners at the finest restaurants in town. Cabo and Cancun had never seen so many "nieces" on all-exclusive packages.

Single women could enjoy casual sex outside of wedlock with no stigma attached. Many women were smart enough to exploit this newfound opportunity, and that awareness, coupled with the ever-present traditional thinking that men should pay anyway, paved the way for a new generation of self-serving feminine financial planners. The what-have-you-done-for-me-lately player was born, and there was one for every macho sucker out there.

Playing the "I'm just a girl with no money" gig while they banked their own earnings, these clever femes sole determined quickly enough that the men were either too horny or too stupid to figure it out, and they were no doubt correct on both counts. Mantras such as, "He who dies with the most toys wins," echoed from the mouths of boastful guys who believed they were the true masters of the universe. As a result, the classic tag line, "Who's your daddy?" became an esoteric irony representing the diminishing state of the once all-powerful patriarchy.

Men continued to step up and spend, believing that pocket charm works every time. And the women, after generations of playing defense, subservient to male breadwinners, finally entered the game playing their own brand of offense. And they were playing it very well, proving that the way to a man's heart was no longer exclusively through his stomach.

Today more women are graduating from college than men. Women make up better than 50 percent of the U.S. workforce, and a significant percentage of women are in higher-earning, more professional positions than their male partners. They may be single women living alone, earning more than the guys they're dating, or married women earning more than their spouses.

Twenty-first-century women can now qualify for their own car loans and home mortgages without any help from men. In many cases, they even have better financial resources and credit than their men. Make no mistake, however, the old barter system is still very much alive and well, but with one key enhancement for women. They can still use sex as a means to getting their bills paid, but with the plus that since they also are earning their own money, they can add to their bank accounts while they're doing it.

Secret No. 12 that men think but don't tell women is, *"Women can fork over some scratch once in a while too."* Spending money isn't a function of gender; it is a medium of exchange. Being born male doesn't mean that by default he is required to pay for everything. Money is merely used to acquire goods and services, regardless of gender. Since women earn money, they can pay for dinner and a movie sometimes, too.

Chad, a thirty-nine-year-old car dealer from Marietta, Georgia, says he's getting tired of being seen as a cash register. "I'm beginning to believe that women think anybody with a penis in his pants is automatically supposed to be their personal bank. I was on a second date with a woman who I know makes at least seventy grand a year, and she asked me how much money I make. And she pressed me about it too. She told me she wanted me to take her to a Falcons game one night and to an upscale restaurant and dancing another. All she was interested in was what I did for a living and how much money I earn. I got the real feeling she just thinks since I'm a guy, I'm paying for her fun tickets pure and simple, and she wanted to make sure I had the amount of scratch she required."

Chad's telling us what a lot of men think but simply won't say. They know women are earning money and understand how to manage it. What bothers them so much is how unfair it is when women who work and make good money still expect men to foot the bill. Frankly, men are tired of being told, "That's the way it's supposed to be."

Ralph, thirty-five, is an IT manager from McKinney, Texas. He says he just doesn't get it. "I just don't understand the deal with women anymore. I can see where men used to pay for everything when women didn't work. I get that. But I keep meeting women who make plenty of money. In fact, a lot of them make more than I do, but they still say that if we're on a date it's my responsibility to pay. Why does it still have to be that way?"

Ralph asks precisely the right question. Why are men still expected to pay? There really is no logical explanation. That kind of thinking is as antiquated as the idea that women shouldn't work outside the home. Maybe women should stay in the home and out of the workplace. After all, isn't *that* the way it's supposed to be?

Whether the check is split fifty-fifty or I'll-buy-this-time, you-buy-next-time, "our" money should be comprised of both his *and* hers. Guys could benefit from a new understanding of women's roles by adopting a "Who pays?" or even a "Let her pay" protocol. It's also time they wake up and smell the coffee cans the girls have hidden in the kitchen cabinet.

Men need to realize that their egos are costing them money. As long as they continue to believe that the thickness of a man's wallet is directly proportional to his success in the dating game, women will continue to let them believe it. And while the guys are busy constantly measuring their manhood, the girls will continue to expand their already swelling bank accounts. And people say size is no indication of performance.

15

POCKET CHARM WORKS BOTH WAYS

Secret No. 13: "Couldn't they at least *offer* sometimes?"

In the past, women didn't have the option to ante up for two very good reasons. First, they didn't have money. Second, paying would have been considered both unfeminine of women and emasculating to men, even if they did have money.

The time has come for an epiphany. Both genders can adopt a new standard where the balance of economic power shifts to a more egalitarian model. And with that shift, it should be understood and accepted that women can also pay for the things that traditionally were paid for by the men. In other words, pocket charm works both ways, and it wouldn't hurt for the guys to start asking the girls, "What have you done for *me* lately?"

Such an attitude shift needs to begin at home. Young girls can be taught a new protocol long before they enter junior high school. They need to grow up understanding that contributing their financial share is both acceptable and normal behavior for women. By the time girls are in high school, moms and dads need to have trained their lovely homecoming queens to show up with the necessary bones to pay for the homecoming king's burrito at Taco Bell.

Teenage girls are already calling boys and asking them out. They're already taunting guys by wearing thongs to school and bending over seductively to pick up their purses. They're even making the first move to jump into the back seat of the Jetta for a spot of heavy breathing. If the tables have been turned regarding these traditional gender roles, the girls can start forking over some legal tender too.

To be fair, not all women are unwilling to pay or to try to do so. But those who do are the exception rather than the rule. And when they kick in their share, it's often their method, how they go about paying, that bothers a lot of men. Since guys have been oriented to be the payers, reversing the role can be somewhat challenging for them. Men wish women would be softer in their approach. They prefer that women respectfully *offer* to pay before impetuously commandeering the check with one hand while waving their platinum card with the other.

Secret No. 13 that men think but don't tell women is, *"Couldn't they at least offer sometimes?"* Most guys genuinely appreciate when a woman takes a turn at paying. It just happens so infrequently that they're not used to it. Plus, it can make them feel like they're not doing their jobs as men. They just wish women would *offer* to pay before grabbing the check without giving them a chance. It's a finesse thing. Corey, forty-nine, a manager from Artesia, New Mexico, believes he represents the way most guys feel.

"When I'm out with a woman, even if it is just a friend of mine, I want to pay. Part of me just wants to be nice, and part of me believes I'm being the proper gentleman I was brought up to be. Still, I like it when a woman pays sometimes, but I really wish she would just *offer* first. Last week I was out with a girl, and when the waiter brought the check, she slapped her credit card down before I could even see it. If she offers first, I can accept and not feel like I'm not being the proper man, but if she just takes charge like that, it makes me feel like less of one."

Trey, thirty-nine, a stock broker from Atlanta, Georgia, says he hasn't dated any "progressive" women, but only the more traditional types. "I have yet to go out with any girl that offers to pay for anything. Don't get me wrong; I like to pay. I think of it as showing respect for the girl. But it would be nice if every now and then, one of them would offer to pay for something, even if it's just a cheap lunch."

By contrast, Ogden, a forty-one-year-old chef from Austin, Texas, says he has experienced what he sees as a role reversal, and he doesn't like it. "My problem is that I try to pay, and the girl pulls out her credit card and one-ups me. She takes charge and gives the waiter her card before I can do anything. I don't like that because it makes me feel like she doesn't think I can pay for it or that she's just showing off. It might be different if she asked me first, but just her taking over like that bothers me, and I won't go out with her again."

Other men say they've had to adjust to it the few times women have actually chipped in. Bob, fifty, a jeweler from Queens, New York, says he had to get used to women paying. "I'm a baby boomer, and I guess I'm from the old school because I expect to pay when I'm out with a woman. So it caught me off guard the first few times a woman offered to pay. But I've come to realize that since they work too, it's okay for them to pay sometimes. I still like to pay most of the time, but I'll admit it's really nice when a woman buys my dinner or treats me to a movie on her dime. It shows me she has class and isn't all about taking advantage of me."

Such generosity doesn't always go unnoticed. Paul, fifty-two, a veterinarian from Lincoln, Nebraska, really appreciates his wife. "Suzie is really great about sharing what she makes from her job to help manage our family money. Plus, she works for General Electric, and they have incredible health benefits, so we are enrolled there, which not only provides us with better coverage than I could have gotten for us as a sole proprietor, but also helps me keep my fixed costs down in my practice."

Stan, forty-seven, a computer programmer from Portland, Oregon, says he thinks women should be commended when they offer to pay, but for a different reason. "I think it's great that women can contribute financially. I tip my hat to those few who do because they're doing that at the same time they're still doing everything else they've always done, like cooking meals, raising kids, and cleaning the house. I don't know too many men who do that."

Stan brings up a great point that a lot of guys miss. Expecting women to share some of their hard-earned cash is both acceptable and progressive. And wanting women to offer first before paying isn't an unreasonable request. But if men want women to break from tradition, men need to be willing to do the same. If wives and girlfriends are going to work full time and share their money just like their male partners, then it's time for the men to ante up their fair share of help around the house. Many women work forty-plus hours each week and still stop on the way home to pick up the groceries, rush back and prepare dinner, clean up afterward, and help the little ones study for their spelling tests.

Meanwhile, the men channel surf as they read the sports page. Old habits die hard. It's time guys learn how to load the dishwasher, polish the stemware, disinfect the porcelain, and hustle the Hoover. And if they're going to continue to leave skid marks in their BVDs, they should also get certified in the general operational methods of using the washer and dryer. Equal is as equal does.

Women are probably better money managers than men. For generations, they've had to learn to stretch every nickel the patriarch tossed them into a dollar. They're hardwired to be frugal, and a penny saved is a penny earned. Over the years, they've honed the skills needed to protect the pesos in their purses.

Still, most women will likely continue to let men foot the bill, and why not? Most men will likely continue to want it that way. But those women who catch on to Secret No. 13 know that *offering* to pay first, rather than assuming the role and trumping their men, will likely pay a better return on their investment. A girl can get to first base with a guy when she pays every once in a while, but she'll hit a grand slam if she *offers* first.

16

WOMEN NEED TO PEEPEE

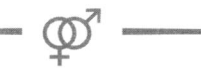

Secret No. 14: "The PEEPEE plan rules!"

Let's revisit Christine and Kevin. Christine has worked for ten years, she does work hard, and she earns her own money. However, while her money is indeed her money—after all, her paychecks are made payable to her—it is the logic she employs regarding the administration and management of it that seems to be leading Kevin's mind into that deepest, darkest jungle of dissonance.

If a woman has the right to spend the money she earns however she wants, on whatever she wants, with or for whomever she wants, why wouldn't a man be entitled to do the same with his money? When money is needed for something jointly shared, like dinner out, vacations, drinks with friends, home repairs, utility bills, pool chemicals, or paint for the hallway *she* wants updated, it makes sense that those expenses be paid from the Our Money account. What doesn't make sense is that the Our Money account contributions come only from his money.

Claiming the right to manage her money as exclusively hers while insisting that Kevin's money must be used for both of them is not only illogical, it most certainly is not fair. And to argue it should be this way because that's the way it's always been is irrational. Frankly, such grossly flawed logic threatens to set the women's movement back forty years.

I admit, had it been me bringing home the brand-new cell phone, the exact sporty little high-tech number she'd been wanting, and had she asked me if I had paid for it, I would have probably teased, "No, dear, I stole it from Best Buy. No one was looking, so I slipped it into my pocket and walked out. At one point the sales girl asked if that was a cell phone in my pants, or was I just glad to see her? Of course, I lied and said I was just glad to see her. Don't worry, she never suspected a thing!"

This is the perfect time for an audit, a financial checkup of sorts, to determine whether Christine and Kevin are practicing an equitable approach to the disbursement of the family funds. They have been kind enough to share an actual accounting of their monthly income and expenses as shown in the table that begins on the next page.

It is important to note that the information that follows may not be appropriate for all audiences. Staunch feminists, traditional stay-at-home housewives and/or mothers, professional men between jobs, and unemployed musicians might find this form of new age accounting offensive.

The Balance Sheet

The following chart represents how money is allocated in Christine and Kevin's family of two. Listed in three columns, the chart provides the income and categorical monthly expenses for Christine under the heading of "Her Money," Kevin's under the heading of "His Money," and the couple's under the column labeled "Our Money."

Gross and net income for them is included at the bottom, along with the remaining net cash available to each at the end of the month. Notice that under the Our Money column, the monthly income is zero, as the income for Our Money is actually the net amount from His Money carried over.

While this chart represents the nature of the financial relationship of specifically one couple in a marriage, reports from others interviewed confirm such an economic arrangement is rather common. John and Suzanne, from San Antonio, Texas, have been married for five years, and they practice this very model. "I make eighty grand a year as a sales manager, and my wife makes forty teaching school. But other than buying groceries, she keeps all of her money, and we use mine to pay for everything else."

Mark and Donna from Santa Fe, New Mexico, agree in principle. "We handle our finances pretty much the same as most people, I think," said Donna. "Since Mark earns more money than I do, we use his money to pay the family bills and for eating out and other entertainment." Mark wouldn't mind if their model were slightly modified. "I wish we could allocate at least half of her money to the family till because it would help me out, but I guess I'm okay with it the way it is, because I take pride in being able to provide for my family."

Let's take a look at Kevin and Christine's arrangement.

Monthly Allocation of the Couple's Financial Resources

Her Money	His Money	Our Money
Her Monthly Income = $7,500	His Monthly Income = $9,500	Their Monthly Income = $0
Her Monthly Expenses	**His Monthly Expenses**	**Their Monthly Expenses**
Her lunch with a girlfriend	Her birthday presents	Their car payments
Her drinks at Girls' Night Out	Her holiday presents	Their car-repair bills
Her panties and bras	Her jewelry	Their vacations
Her cell phone bill	Her vacations	Their monthly household bills

–	Her dates with him	Her clothing
–	Her massages	His birthday present
–	Her facials	His holiday presents
–	Her manicures	Their groceries/toiletries
–	Her credit-card bills	Their mortgage/rent payments
–	His cell phone bill	Their credit card payments
–	–	Their savings account
–	–	Their dinners out
–	–	Their drinks with friends
–	–	Their other recreational activities
After Tax Income = $4,875	After Tax Income = $6,175	Net to Our Money = $4,975
Total Expenses = $709	Total Expenses = $1,200	Total Expenses = $4,975
Net Cash to Her = $4,166	**Net to Our Money = $4,975**	**Net Cash to Him = NOTHING**

Christine saves $4,166 each and every month for a total of $50,000 per year for three years, until she has banked $150,000 plus earned interest. She leaves Kevin, takes a year off from work, lives on less than one-third of her savings, and travels to Cancun with her girlfriends, using a small piece of the settlement money from the divorce. She parades around on the beach wearing the bikini and boob job Kevin paid for, meets Chuck, a muscled-up stock broker from Baltimore, and moves to Maryland.

She marries Chuck, and the game begins all over again, but she's already more than a hundred grand ahead before she sits down to their first dinner as husband and wife. Three years later, she's put more beans in the bank; she divorces and once again hits the sun, sea, and sand to recuperate. Financial planning like that sure beats the hell out of the standard 401K. At this rate, Christine will be retired and financially secure by the age of fifty and still sporting the boobs of a twenty-five-year-old.

Christine's alleged method notwithstanding, women earn more money than ever before, often as much or more than their spouses, boyfriends, or significant others. It logically follows that they can contribute a little something for the coffers; you know, toss a little scratch into the till. In fact, I've come up with a very simple solution to this pressing problem. It's called Proportionally Elected Equal Pay for Equal Earning, or PEEPEE for short. Yes, it's time we all enjoy a good, refreshing PEEPEE.

Spending should all be about proportion. If each individual makes the same amount of money, each of them should contribute 50 percent to the joint expenses. If one earns more than the other, then each should contribute his/her proportionate share.

For example, Kevin earns $9,500 per month, Christine $7,500, for a total monthly joint income of $17,000. Kevin's share of that represents 56 percent, and Christine's the other 44 percent. Their after-tax monthly joint income is $11,050, and their total monthly expenses are $6,884, leaving $4,166 in positive cash flow.

Were they both to pay their proportionate share of the bills, Kevin's cut of the free cash flow would be $2,320, and Christine's $1,846. At this point, each would have their rightful share of money for discretionary spending, and neither of them would be treated unfairly. Should either one want more cash in his or her pocket every month, he or she could take the necessary steps to earn more. As the percentages change, the allocations of expenses and resulting free cash on hand would change proportionately.

Secret No. 14 that men think but don't tell women is, *"The PEEPEE plan rules!"* We can sum this secret up succinctly enough by hearing from Brett, fifty-two, an orthodontist from Burlingame, California. "I earn about four hundred thousand dollars a year from my practice, and my wife earns forty thousand as an elementary school teacher. Still, she covers 10 percent of our total monthly expenses every month. I didn't ask her to do it, she just thinks it's fair, and she wants to contribute something from her earnings. Each of us paying our proportionate share works very well, and we never, and I mean never, argue about who pays for what. I think that proportional pay thing can really work because both people pay for things, but each also gets to keep some of the money earned. It's a great system."

The PEEPEE plan does rule. Women who capitalize on this secret get the best of both financial worlds. They contribute and save proportionally. They know how much of their earned money they will kick in each month and how much they will be able to retain for their own personal use and enjoyment. And they will never be accused of taking advantage of their men.

What Is Good for the Goose . . .

A lot of women are living a rather obvious double standard—not because they are deceptive, devious, and conniving, but because they can. Men are allowing them to do it. Society is allowing them to do it. And, *they're* allowing them to do it. It's nobody's fault. It's just happening naturally because both men and women have, for so long, readily accepted traditional gender roles that dictate men pay for themselves and for women too.

Regardless of the domestic equation, women aren't about to blow the whistle on themselves. Men need to wake up and realize that it's more than a matter of women being predisposed to believe men should pay. It's also about them taking advantage of the knowledge that they can exploit that social convention from yesteryear to their benefit.

In the twenty-first century, logic and proportion in their purest forms would suggest that if his money is somehow our money, then hers is too. Conversely, if her money is exclusively hers, then his money is exclusively his. Long-held social convention notwithstanding, the time has come to right this ongoing wrong. The old "I've got to powder my nose" excuse at about the same time the check arrives is as worn out as the hands on Joan Rivers's makeup artist. Cash and credit cards are accepted, as are personal checks with proper photo ID.

Women know men think they're supposed to pay, and they're not about to flip the box top over and let the guys read the new rules of the game. Something about, "Don't wake a sleeping giant." As long as men allow it to happen, some of the more unscrupulous women out there will continue to drain their men's bank accounts, while they use the money they've earned to stuff the coffee cans hidden in the kitchen cabinet. If guys continue to be disillusioned into thinking they've got to keep laying on the pocket charm, they shouldn't be surprised if some girls keep opting to take a dive into the hip pockets of their pants. And they won't just be copping a feel.

Equal Opportunity Spenders

Women should be given the equal rights they deserve. They should be able to earn money just like men, work in the cube next to men, exercise at the same gym, match men drink for drink at the bar, lead when they dance, initiate sex, and be assertive enough to ask men out. They should also be extended the same privileges the men enjoy when it comes to spending money in a relationship. They should be given the opportunity to contribute their share of the financial load as well. Men really do need to quit denying women their rightful equality.

Men should stop accepting a double standard. They should smarten up and let women pay too. They have the money. In fact, they probably have more than men think. Many of them may even have more money than the men. After all, they've been able to make their money and put it in the bank because they know the guys will be paying for dinner and the movie.

Some people claim women just don't realize how expensive it can be to provide for a date or mate—that they don't understand just how much guys actually spend. Still others believe the ladies know exactly what it takes to support a relationship financially. Joe, a single, forty-four-year-old pilot from Meridian, Mississippi, says he's got it all figured out.

"Listen, women see menus; they know what meals cost. They also know what airfares and hotels cost. I really don't think most of them are about to offer to pay for expensive meals or vacations because they don't want to take that kind of financial hit. They'd much rather let us guys pay for that stuff, and, truth be told, too many of us are too willing to do it, so they know they can take advantage of it. I'm not saying they're maliciously exploiting our generosity, although I'm sure some do, but that they will take advantage of the opportunity. And if we're honest, who would blame them?"

Why haven't women been more vocal about changing this particular, lingering gender-stereotyped behavior from yesteryear? Why are they not spending just as much energy on a quest for equal access to part with their money as they are for equal access into the locker room? Why aren't they just as concerned about achieving equality regarding spending money as they are about earning it?

Maybe in twenty-first century relationships, her money is *her* money, his money is *our* money, and a man better spend *our* money as *she* thinks he should. Otherwise, who knows, she might refuse to play with Mr. Wiggly when he wants her to the most and instead call a friend, go out for a few drinks, and shop for a while—with *our* money.

17

FIRING OFF FINANCIAL PHEROMONES

♂♀

Secret No. 15: "It's a turn-on when the girls pay—sometimes."

The "ante-up" is an aphrodisiac now. There's power in paying, and the sexual tension it creates can be more alluring than Coco Chanel's finest fragrance. Jim, forty-nine, an investment banker from Seattle, Washington, and a confirmed bachelor, says he is turned on when a woman pays her fair share. "Are you kidding? I love it when a woman forks over some scratch. It shows she is confident in herself and comfortable in her skin, and that spells sexy to me. It means she can handle me and take care of herself at the same time. I like that in a woman."

But the aphrodisiac works best if it is an "ante-up-every-now-and-then," not every time. Jeff, a single, forty-two-year-old professional golfer from Palm Springs, California, clarifies and echoes Jim's feelings. "I'm more progressive than most guys, I think, but I actually get horny when a woman takes command of the ship and pays the check sometimes. It pumps me up to know that I don't always have to spend money to get a girl to be into me. I just don't want her to do it all the time."

Secret No. 15 that men think but don't tell women is, *"It's a turn-on when the girls pay—sometimes."* To a lot of guys, there is sexual power in a woman paying. It conveys a form of furtive flirtatiousness. It sends a message that she likes the guy and finds him attractive enough to invest some actual dollars of her own into the connection. And it has an even more powerful affect when she remembers Secret

No. 13, stroking his ego just a bit by showing a little deference while being generous.

Drew, forty-one, a chemical engineer from Bradenton, Florida, says such a personal touch can really get him going. "As a man, I feel more virile, more potent when I can provide for a woman. And though I want to do that most of the time, if a woman takes the right approach and offers to pay for me *sometimes*, especially if I get the feeling she's into me, it can really turn me on. I don't know, it's just something about feeling provided for, like she's really, really attracted to me."

Sam, forty-six, a college administrator from Dallas, Texas, likes that women are willing to part with some cash, as long as it's not too often. "I wish women would pay sometimes just as much as the next guy. And I agree, it can turn me on from time to time. But, I don't want them always to pay. I don't want to feel like a kept man. It works as an aphrodisiac when it happens every now and then. It would have the opposite affect for me if they paid too often."

Guys spend most of their waking hours thinking about sex. They love being turned on, and it really doesn't matter how. As comedian Rodney Dangerfield often said, they get excited squeezing into a tight parking place. The power of a woman can be seductive, and paying the tab can be a powerful seducer. But, much like having sex in their wives' or girlfriends' parents' guest rooms, it's only a turn-on for guys if it is spontaneous and doesn't happen too often.

I was invited to have dinner with a woman recently and talk turned to my book. She said she believes women need *Secrets from Inside the Clubhouse* because they're just as confused as the guys. She claims her sisters across America want to know what guys really think about all of this stuff so they can become, as she called it, "complete New Age women."

She also said that she makes it a practice to offer to pay at least her share when she's on a first date. I found this both refreshing and rather progressive, and of course, since *she* asked me out, naturally looked forward to saving my money this time. For a brief moment, the thought of her paying actually made me feel a tinge of sexual heat. But then she took a sip of wine and added, "Of course, if he doesn't pay for *everything*, he is a wuss, and I'll never go out with him again!"

I finished my meal, cleared the tab, and headed home for a cold shower.

Sports and Superheroes

"So, you guys mind if I work in some reps too?"

18

FEMALE PECTORALIS MAJOR

Secret No. 16: "You can't lift weights— you're a *girl!*"

I make it a practice never to date any woman who can lift more weight than I can. I'm trying to change. I already use all-over body wash in the shower, put moisturizer on my face and hands, clip my nails, and even shop at Nordstrom. I figure I have to draw the line somewhere.

But women *are* lifting weights, and I'm not talking about those cute little five-pounders to tone up their triceps. They're all over the bench press, the seated row machine, and the entire rack of dumbbells. Welcome to the world of the female pectoralis major, Latin for she's-got-bigger-muscles-than-me!

A lot of guys are having trouble digesting this particular phenomenon and several complained to me about it. Allen in particular, thirty-eight, a Web site developer from Huntington Beach, California, was more than slightly embarrassed recently at the gym.

"The other day I was lifting weights, and just as I'm sweating like a pig trying like hell to bench press 225 pounds, some clown comes up behind me and starts yelling, 'DO IT, MAN. PUSH IT! YOU CAN DO IT. IT'S ALL YOU, MAN. IT'S MENTAL. IT'S ALL YOU. DO IT, MAN, DO IT!' I strained to finish my last rep, took a deep breath, and turned to see who the big mouth was. It was a WOMAN! I was humiliated. Then, to make it worse, she stuck her hand up to high-five me and said, 'Great job, man, mind if I work in with you?' I couldn't believe it, a GIRL wanted to work in with me! I didn't know what to do, so I just told her I was finished and she could have it. I had two sets to go, but there was no way I was working out with HER. I'm a guy. She's a girl!"

Women Don't Just Glow Anymore—They Sweat!

Welcome to one of the aftershocks of Title IX. In June of 1972, the Higher Education Act signed into law a mandate to achieve equity in education for both sexes. Title IX of the act paved the way for sports programs in secondary and post-secondary schools to provide girls and women equal access and opportunity to participate. Allen is just a little late to the party. Maybe he was trying to find a parking place.

More than thirty-five years later, women not only lift weights, they also participate in any number of chosen sports, just like the men. They compete in boxing, tennis, swimming, basketball, softball, volleyball, football, and even hiking and fishing, too. In fact, thanks in large part to Title IX, the storied March Madness—for decades the zenith of men's college basketball—now also includes the NCAA championship for women. Apparently, Allen thinks women get their exercise doing aerobics and rolling over in the tanning booth.

Though it may come as a shock to Allen, women are both collegiate and professional athletes. They have the WNBA for basketball, the LPGA for golf, and the WTA for women's tennis. There are also professional organizations for women's soccer, volleyball, and boxing; a few ladies are even competing in the macho sport of car racing. Who could forget Ms. Danica Patrick and her gallant drive toward victory at the Indianapolis 500, anointing her the diva of the IndyCar series?

What Allen no doubt encountered that day at the gym was the weight-lifting version of the new-millennium female athlete. They're working out big-time. Some of them even report actually *sweating!* A lot of folks still think women only glow, but make no mistake about it, they're real athletes. Allen doesn't have to lift weights with them, but he doesn't have to feel threatened because they lift, either. It is what it is, women participate in sports.

I will admit I have seen women like the one who offered to high-five Allen in the weight room. They certainly defy the traditional physical appearance most men expect. I remember one in particular. Her shoulders were wider than mine, her arms were shaped like bowling pins, and her figure could qualify for the centerfold of this year's Trucks-R-Us catalog.

Veins popped from this chick's body like an urban district on a 3-D map! Her arms were so muscular that if she needed to scratch her butt, she wouldn't be able to get her hands back there to do the job! This girl was the size of a Nordic mountaintop and should have had a tattoo on her lower back that said *Peterbilt!* To be fair, she really didn't look any different from most of the pumped-up *guys* in the gym, but that's the point.

Secret No. 16 that men think but don't tell women is, *"You can't lift weights—you're a girl!"* As has been said before, men are visual beings. They have in their heads what psychologists call a series of anticipatory schemata, blue prints of what they think women should look like. The image they have is one of beauty and femininity and doesn't typically look like the Terminator with long hair and a boob job. They want women to look like women, not like men.

Men lift weights to pump up so they can look good to women. They want to be Tarzan to their own version of Jane, and they're not accustomed to seeing her slide a couple of forty-fives onto the barbell and push out three sets of ten. To most guys, pumping iron is a man's sport. If a woman is seen hanging around a rack of weights, she's the girlfriend of some muscled-up Neanderthal at the gym or a bikini-clad babe strolling by a pumped-up group of grunting studs on Venice Beach.

But women have been participating in aerobics classes for going on three decades now, so it shouldn't shock guys to see them extend their routines to include weightlifting. Again, men can adjust, but putting certain established stereotypes to rest can take some time. For example, a lot of guys still think all Asians have black belts in karate. That *isn't* true, is it?

Some guys have a hard time seeing women lifting weights because they think girls just shouldn't do that. To many of them, it's yet another attack on their parochial world. I'm not saying that it's right; I'm just saying that it's real. But just like sands through an hourglass, these are the days of our lives. It can change, it is changing, and it will continue to change. We can do it. We've certainly modified our perceptions of Asians and karate.

Women can capitalize on Secret No. 16 by simply not walking up to a guy doing a set of bench presses and offering to spot him. While guys have developed their muscles, most of them are lagging behind in whipping their cranial areas into shape. Brent, forty, a personal trainer from Dallas, Texas, says he hears about it from a lot of his male clients.

"I've had several guys tell me they know women can work out now too. But they really wish the girls wouldn't lift weights. It's one of those 'guy' things. They want women to be soft and sexy and not build up their bodies. Anyway, I just encourage the women to lift separately from the men. I tell them that if a guy's already using the barbell for instance, let him finish and move on to something else before they use the same equipment. And whatever they do, don't offer to spot a guy or lift weights with him."

Women in the know understand that guys don't have any problem with girls *watching* them lift weights. They just don't want the girls to lift with them. They also know that if they do lift, guys just wish they'd do it for definition, using light weights, just enough to stay trim and toned. They know that men don't want women lifting the heavy stuff to bulk up like a body builder. They just don't think it's feminine. Plus, it could really mess with Tarzan's head if he finds out that Jane can clean and jerk more than he can.

19

TORN TENDONS AND RIPPED ROTATOR CUFFS

Secret No. 17: "Play your own sports and leave ours alone."

Men play golf to get away from women for a while. And you think they just like the game? To a guy, a day on the golf course is an escape from the norm. It's a place where he can go spend time with other humanoids that look and act like him, a place where he can pick his nose and fart and no one will care. The golf course is where he can go and just be a guy. It's the men's version of a day of beauty at the spa.

But golf is a game that can be played by both men and women, separately or with each other. And couples actually do play together sometimes, even *married* couples. When they do share the golf cart, the game is handicapped on behalf of the women to level the playing field by providing them shorter tee shots. A lot of men wish that women would just play with each other, and enjoy the shorter course lengths on their own. So at most public or country club tracks, men tend to play in foursomes with nary a woman in sight.

In fact, many guys believe there are five specific sports that should be reserved for men only. These include the big three: football, basketball, and baseball, plus golf and auto racing. And most baby boomer men in particular think participation in these particular sports is their rightful entitlement. After all, men are bigger, stronger, faster, and more competitive than women—aren't they? Women are supposed to be feminine, not jocks. Jim, forty-five, a real estate broker from Dallas, Texas, thinks women should only participate in "women's" sports and leave the men's alone.

"Baseball, basketball, and football should be for men only. Women should play tennis, softball, and *maybe* golf. And if given the choice, most of us would rather hit the links without the girls, too. They shouldn't be driving on the NASCAR circuit either. They can swim and do gymnastics, and a few of those other non-sports sports, but I'm really getting tired of them invading ours."

Forty years ago, high school girls were the cheerleaders at the football games; today they're some of the players. Four decades ago, the only women who walked onto the hardwoods at a professional basketball game were the players' wives or a fan trying to win a prize during the halftime show. Today they have the WNBA (Women's National Basketball Association), an entire league just for women. They even have their own specially-sized balls!

Four decades ago women watched men race cars; today they're driving them. And though they haven't as yet stepped between the lines on the baseball field, they're donning their cleats in record numbers to pitch the softball and competing head-to-head with the men on both the golf course and the race track.

Charlie, forty-four, an engineer from Tulsa, Oklahoma, said he thinks if women want to compete with men, they should have to compete straight up, with no adjustments or handicapping to provide an advantage for the women.

"I think if women want to play the same sports as men, they should have to play by the same rules. They should have to use the same size ball and three-point-shooting distance as the men in basketball. They should tee off from the same tee boxes as men in golf, and they should be playing baseball instead of softball, with the same field configurations, distance between bases, and pitcher's mound to home plate. If they really think they can do anything men can do, then they should be held to the same standards. Either that or they shouldn't play men's sports."

Charlie's quite the liberated man. I didn't ask him, but I wondered if he thought women should take showers with the men after the game, too. Now *that* would be egalitarian. Wayne, a fifty-one-year-old editor from New York City says he refuses to watch any women's sports programs on TV and skips past any reports printed in the newspapers about them. "I'll say it straight up. Women shouldn't be playing men's sports. I don't like it, and I'm not about to support it. Why must women do every single thing we do? I just wish we could keep something for ourselves, something that makes us different."

Scott, fifty-five, a pharmacist from New Haven, Connecticut, agrees. "I don't follow any women's collegiate or pro teams, and basically look the other way when it comes to any athletic event or sport involving females other than the *Sports Illustrated* swimsuit issue."

Several men who know about Title IX were adamantly against it on the grounds that it has depleted the funds available for athletic scholarships for boys. They provided examples of their own sons receiving only partial scholarships or none at all after being told no more money was available because it had to be allocated to the women's programs. Jason, a forty-nine-year-old sales rep from Plano, Texas, doesn't like to be reminded of what happened to his son.

"My eighteen-year-old was a stud on the baseball field, and one of the stars of his high school team. We thought he had it made for college, and he was getting a bunch of D-1 (NCAA Division I) scholarship offers. But when it came time to sign, he received only a third of a full scholarship because the team only gets around twelve full ones each year now that a bunch of money has to go to the girl's programs so they can play softball. The twelve they have are divided up among around thirty players. I'll be very honest with you, because the girls are getting to play, we really feel like our son got ripped off."

Secret No. 17 that men think but don't tell women is, *"Play your own sports and leave ours alone."* To a lot of men, women have already taken over the household, taken charge in the bedroom, and infiltrated the workplace. They even make up the majority of students on college campuses. And while the guys seem willing to take all of that in stride, they believe sports, at least "men's" sports should remain in the fraternity of men, no girls allowed.

Most guys have no problem with women figure skating, swimming, or straddling the balance beam. After all, to the typical guy, those aren't really sports. But if it involves some kind of a ball or an engine and a set of tires, a lot of guys think women should watch from the bleachers with a diet coke and a bag of popcorn, not actually suit up and play.

But what exactly is the problem men have with women sharing their passion for sports? And is Title IX really so bad? Maybe we're missing something here. Truth be told, the majority of men don't actually play sports anyway. They watch them on TV. Maybe men fear women will want to watch sports on television too, just as they do. It's enough women now *play* and worse when they compete against men. But it would be a travesty if women actually started watching on TV, too. What men really fear is the potential competition for the remote!

It may be time for the guys to take a chill pill and relax. Women are not invading men's sports. They are not campaigning to compete head-to-head against them either, nor are they suggesting that men's programs be eliminated or compromised in any way. They simply want their own sports and their own teams because they, just like the guys, want to play. With rare exception, the vast majority of women *don't* want to compete against men. And the best news for guys is that most women don't give a rat's ass about the remote.

In the '30s and '40s, Babe Zaharias went head-to-head against men in basketball, golf, and even shooting pool. A few decades ago

Billie Jean King faced off against Bobby Riggs in a battle of the sexes on the tennis court, and more recently Annika Sörenstam, Michelle Wie, and Danica Patrick have competed against men in their respective sports. But out of the tens of thousands of women participating in sports, is it really fair to indict *all* of them when proportionally only a handful have been the ones to compete against the men?

Women like sports, too, and want to have their own programs so they can compete and enjoy the benefits of healthy competition and accomplishment just like the men, and why not? Why shouldn't they be able to experience the thrill of victory and the agony of defeat, too? Why shouldn't they be allowed to compete and enjoy both the physical and psychological benefits that come with participation: lessons learned about working as a member of a team, sharing a vision, and the value of preparation? And women should be allowed to have torn rotator cuffs, pulled groins, ripped tendons, and knee surgeries just like the men, too!

Women wise to Secret No. 17 know that having a penis isn't a prerequisite to participating in sports. They understand that there are no "men only" sports, and they ignore the sexist complaints from guys and suit up anyway. Men just need to get over it and enjoy watching the women. I know I do. Some of those Russian tennis players have got me squeezing fuzzy balls and looking for my racket!

20

ROBBING PETER TO PAY PAULA

Secret No. 18: "Hey, that money belongs to us!"

In the quintessential guy flick *Caddyshack*, high school graduate Danny Noonan is desperate for money. It is summertime and his last chance to earn the needed beans for college. He works at Bushwood Country Club as a caddy. Bushwood is awarding a college scholarship to the most deserving louper, and Danny is determined to win it. But his efforts to schmooze the clubs' founder, pompous Judge Smails, fail repeatedly. The judge isn't buying his transparent attempts to suck up and mocks, "Well, Danny, the world needs ditch diggers, too!"

Love Can't Buy Me Money

There may be more than just the male ego at play regarding the participation of women in sports, especially at the collegiate level. Just as with Danny and Judge Smails, emotions often heat up when money is involved, specifically college scholarship money. Many weekend warrior types, erstwhile high school and college athletes themselves, vicariously live through their sons' on-field or on-court performances and pray for the financial assistance that athletic scholarships can provide. Since the passage of Title IX, such subsidies have been made available for women's sports too, diluting the total funds available for young men.

When a father like Jason finds out that the blood, sweat, and tears his son has poured into his chosen sport for most of his life may be rewarded by only a partial scholarship at best, he's none too happy. Realizing that the inordinately long daily practices, the sacrificing of nights and weekends for games, tournaments, or even more practices, and the otherwise missed activities and events of a "normal" childhood result in only a fraction of what it takes to pay for a college education can be heartrending. And to find out that the scholarship award is minimal in large part because the needed funds have been allocated for girls' programs instead, leaves no wonder why a dad like Jason is complaining.

Boys all over America toil away day after day, working toward earning college scholarships and dreaming of one day making it to the pros, only to discover their efforts have been spent in futility because there are at best only limited, or worse, no funds available. A lot of the dads believe that had Title IX never been passed, their sons would be matriculating to university life, the beneficiaries of the very funding they are being denied, financial assistance that for many of them may be the only means accessible for a college education. But would that be fair?

While it is true that Title IX served as the impetus to provide more scholarship dollars for women's programs, and it could be reasonably argued that by default it depletes the resources available for the men, it is actually less an injustice to the men and more a correcting of a long-standing injustice to the women. The parents of girls would love to see their daughters, who also dream of college scholarships or making it to the pros, receive free educations just as much as the parents of boys.

What about the dad who had visions of raising sons and teaching them how to play baseball, but instead has daughters? Shouldn't he have the opportunity to play catch with them or take them to the park for batting practice, just as he would have done had he sons? Girls can benefit from tossing the ball with Dad too. And since more women are now attending and graduating from college than men, couldn't the argument also be made that more funding should be provided for the girls than for the boys?

Girls also toil for years, day in and day out, honing their skills, working to improve, investing the majority of *their* lives practicing and practicing to earn scholarships one day. Shouldn't they be given equal opportunity to earn their way through college, playing the sport of their choice, just like the boys? Talk about equal pay for equal work.

Achieving the success needed to earn a college scholarship has always been a competitive undertaking. Nothing has changed in that regard, and in fact, scholarship money is still available. But since the overall pool of resources must be doled out to activities for both genders, in some of the sports such as baseball, soccer, volleyball, or swimming, it is true that a well-deserving male athlete now may receive only a partial award.

For example, a spot on the roster of the baseball team that might have earned a full scholarship thirty-five years ago will typically receive only a quarter or a third of that amount today. Since the total number of scholarships for the men's baseball team has been reduced, and the team still needs the same number of players, the award per player is naturally less. But a critical point here is that the same scenario plays out for the girls too. Since the sum total of resources available for athletic scholarships is a finite amount, both the boys' *and* the girls' teams must stretch the dollars as far as they can to fill their respective rosters.

There's Just Got to Be a Better Way

Solving the problem of limited funding for scholarship athletes is doable. A simple resolution could be to recognize that the big two, football and basketball, could be treated as farm systems for the pros and receive their funding from the professional leagues and corporate sponsors. This would then allow the dollars currently being granted players in those sports to be available for the other sports in colleges and universities.

Another solution would be to pay coaches of the big two sports more reasonably, thus freeing up still more money for student athletes. Many Division I football and basketball coaches earn more than a million dollars a year coaching their sports, some several million a year. Were they to be paid the paltry sum of, say, three hundred thousand a year, more than what many corporate executives earn, the coaches would still be very well paid for their work, while additional money would be available for students. Coupling the savings realized from payroll with corporate sponsorships and contributions from professional teams, there would collectively be *millions* of additional dollars in the till for scholarships.

Consider this example. Assume that the cost of a college education averages $50,000, or $12,500 per year. Imagine that two million dollars could be garnered each year per school from the contributions of professional leagues, corporate sponsorships, and payroll adjustments. This is not an unreasonable amount in today's market. One hundred and sixty additional full scholarships could be awarded to deserving student athletes. Yes, that's one hundred and sixty scholarships *per year, per school!*

Many men, however, still feel the current system is unfair. A lot of them are adamant in their belief that since the men's programs are the ones providing the lion's share of the revenue most colleges and universities enjoy from their sports programs, more funding should be available for the male athletes. When confronted with the fact that even with the passage of Title IX, the men's programs actually still receive a larger piece of the financial pie than the women's, these same guys argue that the men's programs are still being shorted by default—simply because the women get anything at all.

One group of five fathers of baseball players I spoke with cited the following example about girls' softball to make their case. Bill, the most vocal of the group, made the point for all of them. "In school districts nationwide, money has been provided for the construction of softball fields specifically for the girls' teams to use. As a result, girls now begin playing softball in elementary school to get good enough to one day play at the varsity level in high school. The players good enough to make the varsity team in high school then work toward earning a scholarship to play in college. Thanks to Title IX, money is then allocated for women's softball teams at colleges and universities, which takes that same money away from the men's baseball teams, resulting in only partial scholarships for our boys. Guys like Jason and me believe our sons are getting screwed out of money they rightfully deserve."

Numbers Don't Lie—Just Ask the Government

Well, guys, now that you put it *that* way, I guess it all makes perfect sense. NOT! Girls and women should have the same right to participate in sports as boys and men. If we are of egalitarian mind, how can anyone even question that? Remember, it is not really about competing with men, but about women having an equal opportunity to participate and compete specifically in their *own* programs.

The United States Department of Education's Office for Civil Rights (OCR), the organization responsible for investigating complaints alleging discrimination in the awarding of athletic scholarships, clarifies the actual intent of Title IX. The regulations put forth under the act provide that, *"The total amount of scholarship aid made available to men and women must be substantially proportionate to their [overall] participation rates at that institution."* If this policy is being enforced, could the fathers of male athletes be correct? Could males be receiving unjustly less scholarship money precisely because it is now going to the females instead?

U.S. Department of Education data indicates that for the academic year 2003–2004, of the 494,000 athletes who competed in collegiate sports programs, 59 percent were male and 41 percent were female. Of note is that for the same school year, women represented 55 percent of full-time undergraduate students enrolled at colleges and universities across America, leaving only 45 percent men.

Clearly participation rates did not mirror enrollment rates. According to the parameters of Title IX, 41 percent of scholarship funding should have gone to the women's programs, since only 41 percent of the actual athletes were female. However, many proponents of Title IX don't fully understand the subtle difference between *participation* and *funding* opportunities and would cry foul on the grounds that the women's programs should have received 55 percent of the scholarship funding. Is that fair? Should one gender be given the majority of the funding while comprising less than half of the participants?

Secret No. 18 that men think but don't tell women is, *"Hey, that money belongs to us!"* A lot of men believe women are being awarded scholarship money unfairly. Dustin, a varsity baseball player at Texas A&M believes he received less money than a lot of the girls on the school's softball team.

"I have three or four good friends on the softball team, and they all told me they got full rides (100 percent scholarships). I only got a thirty (30 percent award), and my Dad had to pay for the rest. I think that's unfair because we bring more fans to the games and make more money for A&M than they do. For some reason, the girls get more money than the boys."

Whether parity exists in the awarding of college scholarship money is no doubt a subject ripe for debate. One could argue that if the men's sports programs are garnering the lion's share of the revenue universities enjoy, they should be rewarded for it accordingly in the amounts allocated for scholarships.

By contrast, if the real purpose of scholarship funding is to subsidize education, it could be argued that the number of students benefiting from the awards is more important than the fiscal success of any given sports enterprise. Women who value knowing secret No. 18 recognize the difference and forge ahead because to them the education gained at the end of their college career is more important than what it says on the scoreboard at the end of a game.

But what about the guys who value education too? Lloyd, twenty-nine, a musician from New York City, says he lost his opportunity for a quality education when he was offered a minimal swimming scholarship.

"My parents took me to swimming practice every morning at six o'clock for ten years so I could compete when I got to high school and college. I was All-District in the 50-meter freestyle and finished fourth in the state in the 400-meter relay. But I was offered only a two thousand dollar scholarship because the girls' programs got money too! My parents couldn't afford to pay the difference, so I ended up at a community college and took up music."

Well, Lloyd, the world needs guitar players too.

21

THE THRILL OF VICTORY AND THE AGONY OF DEFEAT

Secret No. 19: "Playing against women just isn't fair."

Maybe there are more women than most of us think who want to exploit their femininity rather than their athleticism. Pitching softball or horseshoes could put the hurt on those French-manicured fingernails in a heartbeat. And most women know that most men are more attracted to them when they're wearing a thong and a lace push-up than a jock and a steel-reinforced, heavy-duty sports bra.

Daddy, I Don't Wanna Play!

Statistics reviewed as recently as March 2007 indicate an inversely proportional relationship between enrollment and number of athletes by gender. Women now make up 57 percent of college student populations, but only 43 percent of the athletes. The total number of female participants still remains well below the comparable proportion relative to the total number of females enrolled in school. By the end of 2004–05, NCAA member institutions averaged 213 (57 percent) male and 160 (43 percent) female student athletes per campus.

Could the disparity between the number of male and female college athletes be due to a lower level of interest among the girls? Could it be that they want to fit the more traditional definition of a college coed? Maybe they simply don't want to try out for the teams.

In traditional sex-role typology, women typically were not as competitive as men when engaged in sports, in large part because they would be perceived as not being feminine.

There are exceptions, of course, but most women have been brought up to be more relational, more filial with one another, and many of them may not be interested in participating in the kind of rigorous, bloodthirsty competition most collegiate sports demand. Interestingly, when they do play, some of them demonstrate a keen interest in socializing or helping each other, rather than setting their sights on destroying one another.

When high school girls are observed competing in softball or basketball games, and play stops because one of the girls takes a spill or gets hurt, not only her teammates but a few of the girls from the opposing team can often be seen helping her. And when the game is over, though they may have been battling against one another on the field or court, members from both teams can be seen in small groups together, laughing, hugging each other, and talking like sorority sisters having a slumber party. For a lot of girls, the ultimate competition between them takes place less on the field and more in front of the locker room mirror.

Guys versus Girls?

Should men and women compete against each other? If they did, the girls might actually have an advantage. They could exploit their not so secret weapon. We've all heard that sex sells. Secret No. 19 that men think but don't tell women is, *"Playing against women just isn't fair!"* Women can use their looks to exploit the unfair advantage they know they already have. The second a typical guy lays his eyes on a beautiful girl, the contest appeals to his *other* mode of masculinity, and he totally loses the killer instinct needed to compete.

Imagine Scarlett Johansson, Penelope Cruz, and Beyoncé Knowles in string bikinis, their tanned skin glistening in baby oil under a tropical sun. Enter three strapping, athletic guys. Now, tell them to go one-on-one against each of the girls on the basketball court. The instantly disadvantaged studs will cry uncle faster than Mel Gibson at a MADD awards banquet.

For a lot of guys, competing against girls just isn't fair because they were taught to compete *for* women, not against them. Most men have been oriented not to take advantage of women—specifically *not* to win—and in fact, to let the ladies win. Boys are told it simply isn't polite to beat girls. And ultimately, guys can't win, no matter the actual outcome of the contest anyway. Should they claim victory, they're admonished for beating the girls. Yet if the girls win, the guys are mocked and humiliated for losing to them.

Doug, a forty-two-year-old salesman from Seattle, Washington, says he knows exactly how it feels. "When it comes to sports, I don't like to compete with my girlfriend because the way I see it, I can't win. If I do win, then I feel like I bullied her, and if I don't, then I feel like I'm less of a man. Plus, my friends and family will give me all kinds of grief either way. They'll bust me for beating her or bust me for losing to her. Seriously, I can't win."

Phil, thirty-three, a pilot from Bloomfield, New Jersey, thinks it's no contest when faced with competing against a woman. "I can't do it. I can't go toe-to-toe against a girl. To tell you the God-honest truth, if I know I can beat her, I feel guilty as hell for even trying. But to think I could lose makes by balls tingle. It just isn't fair, and we shouldn't have to do it. I mean, a man's got to be a man, and face it, he can't be much of a man if he's playing against a woman!"

But with rare exception, women are competing against other women, not against men. Maybe guys should think of the *advantages* of women playing sports instead of seeing it as a threat to their manhood. It might improve the odds of them being able to watch more ESPN. It might give them and their significant others more to talk about. It might even get them more fun tickets to punch with their buddies, now that their ladies have a better understanding of the benefits derived from playing or watching sports. And if the wives and girlfriends start working out and competing too, they may stay in better shape. Think about what it could do for wet T-shirt contests!

Equal Play for Equal Work—Maybe Guys *Should* Compete Against Girls

Let's not forget about the all-important crusade for egalitarianism. Women, most notably the feminists, have long been advocates for true equality between the sexes. And now that girls can play on boys' teams, surely it won't be long before the guys get to play on the girls' teams, right? Think about how much fun that could be. It could redefine the entire concept of touch football. First there was spin the bottle, then Twister; soon guys could be pinning a flag on some curvaceous posterior and copping a feel in the open field.

Certainly the feminists wouldn't charge the hill pushing for girls to have the right to play with guys unless they were willing to afford the guys equal opportunity to play with the girls, would they? Multiple campaigns have been waged to allow girls to play on boys' baseball teams. Accordingly, boys should be allowed to play on girls' softball teams too, right? They would never suggest that boys could not join girls' teams, would they? They couldn't admit that guys are bigger and stronger than girls. That might suggest the guys have an advantage. And that kind of thinking would be sexist!

Stranger things have happened. One group of women has actually come forward complaining that men should not be allowed to stand to urinate because it represents a showing of superiority over women.

I swear I didn't make that up, it really happened. So now women are discriminating against men in, of all places, the restroom? Wow, simply because they were born male. Talk about penis envy!

Maybe it's time for equal play for equal work. If men and women should play by the same rules in the workplace, maybe there should be a true leveling of the playing field in sports too. For example, why do women use a smaller basketball than men? Some might suggest it's because their hands are smaller. Were that true, one would think the women would have trouble handling the much larger softball while the men with bigger hands complete with a much smaller, harder baseball.

Has the time come for the NBA champions to take on their counterparts from the WNBA in a best-of-seven series? Or LeBron James and Lisa Leslie could stage a roundball battle of the sexes. And what about softball and baseball? Jennie Finch could try pitching to Manny Ramirez. Now that would really level the playing field.

In golf, the shorter tee shot represents the only difference in the way the game is played between women and men. Country club and public golf courses measure the same distance from tee to green regardless of the gender of the players. Why are women given any advantage at all?

Should Tiger Woods be allowed to compete in an LPGA tournament? Annika Sörenstam got to play in a PGA event. It would be like-for-like, the best man and woman in the sport swapping places for a tournament. Not conceding such a proposed match for whatever reason seems sexist. It provides women an advantage by default.

The pedal to the metal in a race car yields the same results regardless of the gender of the foot that pushed it. Yet no male first-time winner has been afforded anywhere near the same celebrated, conquering-hero status, nor the lucrative endorsements, Danika Patrick enjoyed after she garnered her first win. Was it so spectacular that she won or that she simply got behind the wheel? Is professional car racing already guilty of practicing a double standard?

Just Get Over It!

Better yet, maybe women and men should just stick to their own sports and not compete against each other. Maybe women should compete only against other women, and men against other men. Each gender could have its own sports, with its own leagues. Maybe the only real crossover could be in the fan base for the two. Each could watch their own contests; plus, women could watch men's sports and men could watch women's.

Women up to speed on Secret No. 19 know that men aren't accustomed to competing against women in sports, so they don't promote it. Instead, they enjoy playing sports with other women and encourage their men to compete against other men. They also know that supporting their guys, rooting for them, and sharing the joy of victory and the agony of defeat not only don't compromise their womanhood, but can actually strengthen their relationships with men.

In time, men like Doug and Phil will likely come around and accept that women can have an equal opportunity to compete in sports. But that doesn't mean they must compete against men. Still, if girls can play on boys' teams, maybe the day will come when the boys will be playing on the girls' teams. Who knows? Sports could become as metrosexual as fashion.

Maybe the WNBA will merge with the NBA, the size of anyone's balls notwithstanding. Maybe the LPGA will merge with the PGA, the length of the tee shots becoming a non-factor. And maybe any first-time winner of a professional car racing event, regardless of gender, will be glorified, celebrated, get a big endorsement deal, and make the cover of *Sports Illustrated* with or without a bikini.

Right, and Woody Allen will be wearing a rhinestone thong on the cover of the next swimsuit issue.

But wait a minute. I'm confused. Who would stand or sit to urinate? Should we install pink porcelain receptacles on the walls in the women's restrooms? Oh, that's right, no doubt all the urinals would have already been removed from the men's restrooms, just to make it fair.

22

IT'S A BIRD! IT'S A PLANE! IT'S . . . A WOMAN!

Secret No. 20: "Be like a Bond girl, not one of Charlie's Angels."

Butch, a beleaguered thirty-nine-year-old bartender from Boston, Massachusetts, isn't buying women in the role of superhero. "My girlfriend dragged me to the dollar movies the other day. I thought we were going to another chick flick. But when the movie came on, it was called *Underworld*, and it was all about some leathered-up hot babe whipping a bunch of different guys' asses over and over again. She's wearing skin-tight black leather pants and a leather vest with her boobs hanging out the top. Don't get me wrong, *that* part I liked. But seeing her kicking ass, one guy after the next, was ridiculous. Do you actually expect me to believe that could happen in real life? Now *women* are the superheroes doing the ass-kickin' of men? I'm really bent out of shape about this!"

I wonder if Butch the bartender is getting paid every time he uses the word "ass." Anyway, not since Wonder Woman or the original Catwoman in the old *Batman* TV series has there been such a presence of female superheroes. Butch is right: today's superhuman vixens are doing some serious butt-kicking! Oh, should I have said ass-kicking?

Conventional manhood is being taken to task like never before, and it's raising a lot of eyebrows and some inquisitive questions. For example, how, in the 2003 big-screen remake of the popular seventies television series *Charlie's Angels* could the rather buxom Drew Barrymore perform a triple cartwheel across a bullet-laden warehouse while under fire, then drop a manly warrior three times her size and five times her strength to his knees with one masterful kick, all while being called an "angel" and tending to her eyeliner?

In another woman-hear-me-roar flick, Angelina Jolie played Lara Croft, who looked more like a brunette Barbie doll than a tomb raider, but she could leap tall buildings in a single bound. And from 2001 to 2006, girl-next-door type Jennifer Garner may have been both stealthy and sly, but she looked as if her real alias could have been homecoming queen. Meanwhile, another leading lady of sorts, our good friend Rosie O'Donnell, continues to prove just how much of a son her father had and how much of a man she grew up to be!

The American female has evolved from the damsel in distress, the coy kitten, to a whole new breed of cat, and a lot of them believe they should be crowned the undisputed champions in the battle of the sexes. And speaking of Rosie, imagine what would happen if she squared off in the ring toe-to-toe with her arch nemesis, the Donald. The only parity possible in that fight would happen at the weigh-in.

If it's any consolation, I'm bigger than Laila Ali, but I guarantee you I'm not about to sign up to be her next opponent in the ring. And besides, I thought size was no indication of performance. But while Butch could use some charm-school classes, he is not alone in his thinking. A lot of guys are tired of seeing tattooed musclemen laid out on their backs, bloodied and beaten by some hot chick in a halter top.

When society at large thinks of warriors engaged in battle, most folks don't picture girls camouflaged in fatigues firing bazookas. Even today, four decades after the feminists made their pitch to rid the world of men, the front line on the battlefield is still, for the most part, the province of the male soldier. And though we have the exceptional types like Ms. Ali, most women still prefer for the men to do the fighting, not just in times of war but whenever and wherever there is a call for physical conflict.

Butch and his cohorts have been conditioned to accept the warrior role since early in their lives. Commands like, "Be a man, damn it!" and "Gut it up!" or "Suck it up and get in there and fight, fight, FIGHT!" have served as succinct colloquial calls-to-arms since before those men were in junior high. Guys grew up being told over and over that big boys don't cry, and they were encouraged, even expected, to be strong, face trouble head-on, and not back down. For Butch and many other men like him, watching one of his brothers-in-arms physically bested, downed, humiliated, and beaten by a woman is both difficult to witness and hard to accept.

But *Underworld* is just fictional entertainment, not a factual report from some journalist covering the beat. Guys should relax and take it for what it is, just a show. Besides, I've seen that movie, and I'd watch Kate Beckinsale underworld, overworld, or anywhere around the world for that matter. My advice to any guy struggling with this shocking trend is to close your eyes, take three very deep, slow breaths, and chant silently to yourself, "It's only a movie. It's only a movie. It's *only* a movie."

Hollywood's New Take on the Leading Man

In addition to women playing superheroes in the movies, on TV they're often portrayed as the smartest ones in the office and at home, too. Lynette routinely outsmarts her husband Tom in *Desperate Housewives*, even besting him in running the fledgling pizza joint he started after he needed *her* permission to open it. And Sarah ran the family business in *Brothers & Sisters*, even though Dad had groomed one of her three brothers to take over before he died.

Dr. Cristina Yang is the smartest of the bunch of interns on *Grey's Anatomy*, flying through her final exam while simultaneously preparing for her wedding to take place hours later. Of course Yang wriggled out of both the nuptials and the dress literally at the last second with the groom and best man standing in front of a nearly full church. Meanwhile, back at the hospital, the one intern who failed the exam and has to choose between abandoning becoming a doctor or taking the entire internship over again from the beginning is a *man*.

Cashmere Mafia is a TV series that takes *Sex and the City* for a figurative spin around the block. The girls in this show aren't so much living life in the fast lane while jumping from bed to bed; instead, they're business moguls and power brokers while their men play supporting roles. The messages being sent over and over aren't even subliminal: men are inferior, not as smart, and not as resourceful as women. Men are portrayed as the buffoons, the butts of the jokes, and the inept bumbling idiots in popular television sitcoms and even in commercials. In other words, welcome to the twenty-first century, where *Dirty Harry* now lives life *According to Jim*!

Charlie's Angels first aired on television in the seventies. It was a popular show, but arguably because it captured a viewing audience of both men and women who appreciated more the *looks* of the angels than the true quality of their combat skills and street smarts. Though we never saw Charlie (voiced by John Forsythe), there was never a doubt that the angels were "his girls," a harem of three, not only under his employ, but dedicated to interpreting his every wish as their dutiful command.

When the movie version debuted twenty years later, one major modification to the original story was obvious. *These* angels could do some serious physical harm! They were still plenty good-looking, but their physical appearance was not their number one attraction. *Tomb Raider, Elektra, Catwoman, Ultraviolet, Sin City, Underworld,*

Kill Bill, and others followed, each one a testament to, and showcase for, the female protagonist's raw talents in hand-to-hand combat and fighting smarts, with her physical attractiveness an ancillary bonus.

The men I interviewed told me they were interested in these movies only because they wanted to gape at the gorgeous females, not because they wanted to see them fight. A clear majority of them said they didn't like seeing the women beating up the men, that it made them very uncomfortable.

Stan, forty-four, a single teacher from San Diego, California, doesn't like it at all. "I'll tell you what. I'd have an inferiority complex if a woman beat me in tennis, let alone in a fight. When I see men, especially ripped and buff men like the guys in these movies, getting slaughtered by women, it makes me nauseous. I just can't believe it, and for some reason it really makes me feel threatened."

Patrick, a married, fifty-five-year-old executive from Miami, Florida, understands how Stan can be affected by what he sees. "My wife and I were talking about this, and she asked me how it made me feel. I told her I really didn't care because it was just a fantasy and because I wasn't planning on getting into a physical fight with a woman, anyway. But as a man, I can empathize with Stan. Seeing a woman whipping a man is very humbling and humiliating."

Collin, thirty-five, an anthropologist from Boulder, Colorado, wants these women to be more traditional. "I don't think the public at large really buys into the concept of women as superheroes. And I can tell you this; men want women to be softer, more feminine, more traditional. They don't like it when women are tougher than they are, at least not physically."

Secret No. 20 that men think but don't tell women is, *"Be like a Bond girl, not one of Charlie's Angels."* Men want women to be resourceful, strong, and self-sufficient, but they also want them to be in touch with their feminine side. Contrary to the opinion of some, they really don't want ditzy airheads accompanying them to the company holiday party or out for a special evening on the town. Okay, Hugh Hefner does, but his preferences in women read like samples from the periodic table of elements: platinum, silicon, and uranium, preferably from Berkelium, Californium.

Men prefer women to be able to speak in complete sentences, too. They just don't want women so smart and so powerful that the men don't feel needed. Guys want to fulfill their socially ascribed role as men, and they love women who let them. Men also want to be heroes to women. But it can be hard for guys to be heroic for girls when the girls can kick more butt than they can.

The Bond girls aren't just vacuous babes busting out of barely-there brassieres. They have brains too. And though they are not indomitable physically, they can typically fend for themselves and often rescue Bond himself. Still, they are the epitome of femininity. Halle Berry was pretty darn skilled at defending herself, but she knew how to make an entrance like a classic beauty. No matter how suave Bond appeared while lying in wait, he was like a kid in a candy store the moment he saw her emerge from the ocean and strut her stuff as she approached him on the beach.

Women wise to Secret No. 20 know how to make an entrance. And when they do, they want their men to carry *them* across the threshold, not the other way around. To a lot of men, the most alluring and beautiful women are the ones who let men be men. Guys may watch the Angels because they're hot, but they'd much rather make company with Bond girls because they can still be the heroes they really want to be. Smart women know the real way to a man's heart is to make a U-turn just before the stomach, head two blocks north, and make their ultimate entrance just inside the gate that circles the hamlet known as egoville.

23

DON'T QUIT YOUR DAY JOB

Secret No. 21: "It's okay to look like a superhero... don't act like one."

Women superheroes might not want to quit their day jobs. Domestic box office numbers tell an interesting story. *Spider-Man* grossed more than $403 million dollars. *Spider-Man II* grossed $373 million; *King Kong*, $218 million; *Batman Begins*, $205 million; and *Superman Returns*, just over $200 million. I guess when Superman saw Batman *begin* again, he decided to *return*. Even *Casino Royale*, a recent James Bond flick, grossed over $167 million.

By comparison, *Charlie's Angels* was the only movie with female leads as certified butt-kickers to register triple digits, grossing only a little more than $125 million dollars. *Charlie's Angels: Full Throttle* managed just over $100 million while *Sin City* grossed $74 million, *Kill Bill Volume II* $66 million, *Underworld* $62 million, *Catwoman* only $40 million, and *Ultraviolet* a paltry $18 million. And without Bruce Willis, Clive Owen, and Mickey Rourke in it, *Sin City* might have been painted a few shades darker than *Ultraviolet*.

The Numbers Don't Lie

All the movies starring women as the heroes/superheroes shared two important factors. One, the women were sexy, gorgeous, and resourceful. And two, the dollars they generated paled in comparison to the movies of the same genre with men in the hero/superhero roles. Interestingly, the two *Angels* movies, the only ones to hit three-figure millions, differed from the others in one very significant way; the women were more feminine and were willing to expose their vulnerable sides too.

In 1985, *Rambo: First Blood Part II* grossed more than $150 million; and *Rocky IV*, $127 million. These statistics are in 1985 dollars, yet both movies dwarfed the earnings from the features mentioned above with female heroes/superheroes that were produced more recently. The numbers don't lie, and the story they're telling is clear: the viewing audience prefers to see the men doing the butt-kicking.

With the possible exception of *Charlie's Angels*, the feature films with a woman in the role of the premier man-kicker took a beating at the box office, often losing to the critics by unanimous decision as well. Apparently, it is okay for women to look like superheroes, but they'd better not act like them.

In a largely patriarchal society such as the United States, can we change our collective view? Can women really be superheroes? Can they be faster than a speeding bullet, more powerful than a locomotive, and leap tall buildings in a single bound? And most important to men, can they look hot doing it?

Every now and then even a blind squirrel finds a nut. Maybe they really can do it. I was serious when I said I'm not getting in the ring with Laila Ali. We're creating bigger, stronger females; just check out the typical women's college basketball, softball, or volleyball teams. We should not be surprised to see some of them pull out a can of whoop ass and put the hurt on some otherwise-macho guys.

Maybe it isn't too farfetched to believe that a size-fourteen, six-foot-tall, one-hundred-sixty-pound body-building bombshell appearing sans her thong as the centerfold in some newly created *Popular Eugenics* magazine could also be a superhero capable of saving the world. If nothing else, she could put the hurt on a middle linebacker for sure. But a solitary size-zero, five-foot-five, one-hundred-five-pound chick laying out twenty savage guys, all trained killers twice her size in full battle garb carrying machine guns, in a matter of seconds—*by herself*?

I know these movies are about fantasy, but one key point must be made. The fantasy guys have when they watch a James Bond movie is that *they too* can be the cool, suave, men of the hour, capable of fighting the foe, saving the world, and getting the hot girl, and all without even a wrinkle in their custom Armani suits. It's all about the Ferrari and living life in the fast lane, at least for a couple of hours.

The allure for the guys watching these movies is that they can see themselves in the protagonist. They can identify with Bond, even emulate him. They can't create that fantasy when they're watching some hot, sexy chick who could model for Victoria's Secret, the damsel in distress they envision *themselves* heroically saving, effortlessly cutting down an army of highly skilled hit men, without so much as a broken fingernail.

But if we're willing to concede that women can be superheroes, why don't more women support them? Why don't all women support them? More specifically, why don't these films do as well financially as the ones with the male stars? A lot of women agreed it's a guy thing, that men are supposed to be the fighters, and they, too, can't seem to make sense of women being able to dominate and defeat men so easily. Most women still believe superheroes wear boxers or briefs, not panties and bras, although Christian Bale could probably pull off a thong and some fishnet stockings, provided, of course, they match his cape.

I Want a Man with a Strong Hand

Most women in mainstream America not only expect men to respond in the presence of physical threat, they prefer it that way.

They want a man with a strong hand, and when it comes to fantasy, women overwhelmingly agree that with rare exception, they want to fantasize about male heroes, not female. Portia de Rossi may dream of her hero, Ellen, fending off the intruding Don Juan in the dead of night who unwittingly found his way into *their* bedroom, but the typical American woman fantasizes about being with a man.

Most women want their men to be the tough, resourceful heroes who make it to the train tracks in the nick of time to untie them and rescue them from certain demise. They also know their guys don't mind watching the men in those roles, because they'll just live vicariously through the characters they see portrayed. Most guys can accept the suave, sophisticated man-about-town or the buff and ripped stud as the hero because they see the guy as their macho alter ego, not as a competitor. They fancy themselves the hero saving the damsel in distress, with her falling in love with him as his just reward.

Who Knew Women Had Issues?

Women don't want other women to be superheroes. Were the world to have too many Catwomen, at least two psychological issues might surface. First, women might feel intimidated by another woman so physically powerful and simultaneously sexy. She represents both an unwanted competitor and a potential threat to their safety. The possibility that another *woman* could whip their men, and look better than them while doing it, leaves women feeling unprotected and vulnerable.

Second, it may expose some heretofore never-expressed subconscious sexual desires. Power is an aphrodisiac, and has long attracted women to men. What if a woman were to find herself sexually attracted to Catwoman, Lara Croft, or Xena the Warrior Princess? Such ingredients as beauty and power could combine to create a most seductive Molotov cocktail. It could bring a whole new meaning to the phrase, "Hey good-lookin', can I buy you a drink?"

So this whole female superhero gig grabs hold of the human psyche and plays it like a fiddle. The psychological underpinnings of it affect both men and women. Men fear being humiliated by the prospect of being bested by a girl, and yet they can't take their eyes off her; she's breathtakingly beautiful and appeals to their libidinous instincts. Women lose confidence in how safe they feel with their men, and yet equally can't take *their* eyes off her. They can appreciate both her on-fire hot looks and the sexual allure of her power, and they know she measures off the charts in both.

Most men and women would never admit to any of this, of course; it's a psychological possibility they'd rather leave buried deep in the solitary confines of their subconscious. Since both men and women may likely be at once fearful and mesmerized, maybe the majority of them just avoid confronting these psychological issues by simply not watching. It certainly could account for the anemic box-office results.

Superheroes aren't exactly ideal role models for relationships either. I couldn't help noticing that most of them don't have spouses or significant others. I guess the travel schedule is just too hard on a relationship, and the dry cleaning bills must be astronomical.

Remember—It's Only a Movie

The most important point for us to remember is that these movies are fictional. The girls of *Charlie's Angels*, *Catwoman*, *Electra*, and the other heroines really aren't any less unrealistic in their heroics than Bond, Rambo, or the Terminator. No matter who does the combative gymnastics, men or women, they're wildly nonsensical, totally surrealistic, wholly unbelievable, born and bred of pure fantasy, and far beyond the realm of reasonable possibility. But hey, they're also a lot of FUN! So just sit back and enjoy the ride.

Guys need to chill out and indulge in the simple pleasure of watching hot chicks looking hot in hot outfits in hot pursuit of an enemy that threatens our very existence. Instead of complaining about it, they should be thankful for it. They can take advantage of the opportunity to gape and gawk at flat-of-stomach, firm-of-thigh, big-of-breast super-vixens with their better halves sitting in the seats right next to them, most probably without complaint. Unless you're Pee-wee Herman, I see that as a plus.

In the real world, Catwoman can no more scale the Empire State Building with such effortless grace and ease than can King Kong. Spiderman can't spin his web across the metropolis with any more proficiency than any one of Charlie's Angels, and the Terminator is no more the killing machine than are Ms. Ultraviolet or Lara Croft. The fact that women are now portraying superheroes in the movies just means that Hollywood has become more egalitarian regarding the distribution of the hero roles and now includes women. There are no fewer male superheroes that I'm aware of. The fictional roles have simply been made available to both genders.

Secret No. 21 that men think but don't tell women is, *"It's okay to look like a superhero . . . don't act like one."* Remember, guys may not like the combat skills of these supervixens, but they love the way they look. In *The Fifth Element*, a feature film that starred Bruce Willis, Milla Jovovich stole more than one scene as a wholly different and rather breathtaking version of the babe in swaddling clothes, especially in the scenes where half of the swaddling was missing.

Ms. Jovovich received rave reviews for her portrayal of the alien superhero Leeloo, a breathtaking beauty, supremely feminine, and considered to be the "perfect being," but in dire need of the strength and resourceful heroics of ex-soldier turned cab driver Korben Dallas, played by Bruce Willis. Leeloo is the one remaining at-large element, the fifth element, needed to save the earth and keep ultimate evil at bay for another five thousand years. Her power lies within her beauty, and her ultimate force is found in her femininity. Yet she still needs Korben, a man, to rescue her and deliver her to the one and only spot where she can be positioned to intercept and turn back the forces of evil determined to destroy earth.

The Fifth Element debuted in May of 1997, and grossed more than 263 million dollars. Remember *Ultraviolet*? Ms. Jovovich's other superhero movie, the one where she is kicking men all over the place, debuted in 2006 and grossed a pitiful $18 million, or 7 percent, yes just 7 percent, of the revenue *The Fifth Element* generated. And that's comparing 1997 dollars to 2006 dollars, when ticket prices were substantially higher. Of course, *The Fifth Element* also starred Bruce Willis. Once again, a man was one of the heroes.

Still, if guys *are* going to watch flicks with all-powerful chicks, they shouldn't pay *too* much attention to the superbabes. The women don't particularly want them ogling Halle Berry in a cat suit anyway, and they might suspect something when they get a skintight outfit just like it from Victoria's Secret as an early birthday present the very next day!

Bill, thirty-nine, a married geologist from San Marcos, Texas, says he likes it when his wife dresses like Catwoman. "I don't mind going to those movies where the girl is the superhero. I know it's all a fantasy anyway. I'm okay with my wife looking like one; I just don't want her to try to act like one. And I'll admit, I *love* it when we come home and my wife dresses up in an outfit we call the cat skin—it's a one-piece body leotard thing I bought for her because it makes her look like Catwoman. When she shows up in that outfit, she looks so hot I forget about the movie real fast."

Women wise to Secret No. 21 know how to play the superhero game. They make sure they look like one, and then they let their men act like one. They know the real power of women is in their brains, their beauty, and their femininity—not in their fists. With weapons like that, it takes just one shot to bring a man to his knees.

24

DONNING FATIGUES LIKE THE TRADITIONAL MAN

Secret No. 22: "Get in the foxhole, damn it—you're a girl!"

We've established that men define their manhood through sex, work, and money. We can now add a fourth dynamic often considered an indicator of masculinity: war. Frontline fighting in a war may be the ultimate measure of manhood. And this one is no laughing matter.

Men in America are oriented to the concept of war from an early age. Boys grow up playing army or cowboys and Indians, often emulating and imitating war heroes, both real and fictional. They sit in front of their televisions or computer screens for hours, engrossed in competitive war games, graphic in both the degree of violence and the ensuing outcomes, replete with blood and guts in full Technicolor.

Playing war has become big business too, and the make-believe artillery, especially these days, looks so real there are actual cases on record where police officers have arrested adolescent boys and confiscated their weapons, only to find that the guns were toys. And until President Richard Nixon eliminated the draft in 1973, most boys growing up in America assumed that at the ripe old age of eighteen, they would enter the military and be trained and prepared to fight in times of war to help defend our country.

Girls did not have this concern. Historically, women were not considered candidates for conscription, and even today are precluded by the Pentagon from serving in "combat occupations." They are entering the military in increasing numbers and are eligible to fill some 80 percent of military jobs, but those jobs are in the capacity of combat support, and they are specifically not assigned to infantry, tank, or submarine duty. Why not?

David, twenty, has already been on the front line during two tours of duty to Iraq. He asks the same question. "Why can't women serve with us on the front line? Since I was in junior high school, my parents and teachers have always told me girls can do anything boys can do. I've seen girls in the army, but not one time have I seen one in the heat of the battle. If a girl can do anything I can do, why doesn't she have to fight on the front line too? We can use all of the help we can get."

Tom, sixty-one, a retired postal worker from Dallas, Texas, agrees. "When I was David's age, I was on the front line in Vietnam. There were no women there with us, and we wanted it that way because we wanted to protect women and children. But today I keep hearing about how women don't need men around, that they can do anything any man can do, that they should have the same jobs and get paid the same as men, too. Okay, then they should jump into the foxhole right next to the men, damn it. If we're equal, by God, then we're equal."

David and Tom make very valid points. While women have been proving their merit in wartime since Korea, a transcript from the July 2007 PBS *Online News Hour* reports that as of that date, women had served some 167,000 tours of duty in the wars in Iraq and Afghanistan, more than four times the number in the first Gulf War. But they are not typically serving in the heat of the actual battle itself, with the frontline assignments still being reserved for the men.

Secret No. 22 that men think but don't tell women is, *"Get in the foxhole, damn it—you're a girl!"* A lot of men really believe that if women can go head-to-head with them in the workplace, in sports, at school, and at home, they can take a spot right next to them in battle. Men are tired of the double standard that says women can be their equal where and when they choose but can still elect not to be when it is to their advantage.

Scott, forty-one, a draftsman from Long Island, New York, doesn't mince any words when he describes how he feels. "I'll be very blunt. I'm tired of women bitching about not being treated equally all the time, and then bitching again when someone says they ought to have to fight on the front line in a war. I say if they can run a company or play a sport just like a man, they can fire an AK-47 just like one, too. The gun doesn't know who's shooting it. It just fires when the trigger is pulled."

The role of soldier on the front line, and with it the expected risk of traumatic stress and potential loss of life, has long been considered a valorous endeavor, a masculine undertaking, and the ultimate test of manhood. Understandably, men like David, Tom, and Scott may not appreciate the double standard at play when it comes to the battlefield any more than they can believe that a thin, shapely, sexy feminine beauty looking like the traditional woman—can kick butt like the traditional man. But if she can, they believe she can do it right next to them in the foxhole.

Women who really get it when it comes to Secret No. 22 understand how men might feel about being asked to risk life and limb for their country knowing women aren't being required to do the same. They respect the valor of men. They honor the heroic efforts of men. And, perhaps most important, they genuinely appreciate every single one of the men fighting on their behalf to protect and preserve their freedom, indeed, the very freedom that provides them the right to bitch about gender inequity. Smart women appreciate men for being men, not some homogenized, watered-down, waxed, buffed and puffed, unisexual imitation of one. Those guys won't crawl into the foxhole any more than the women will.

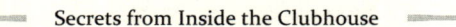

HEAD
OF
HOUSEHOLD

*"Well, he is rough, but with new clothes,
a different haircut, a manicure, a facial . . .
and a little less 'junk-in-the-trunk,'
he may have potential."*

25

TOILET SEATS AND DIRTY UNDERWEAR

Secret No. 23: "Live and let live; don't try to change us."

Apparently Don didn't receive the latest memo from his new bride. She just got promoted! If he did see the memo, he must have failed to open the attachment and read the terms and conditions of the new marriage manual. In section seven, subtitle C of paragraph nine, it clearly states, *"As soon as the vows have been spoken and the ring is placed on her finger, the bride becomes the self-appointed CEO of Our Life Together, Inc., and board meetings will never be the same again."* That boy needs to read his e-mails more carefully.

Don is a forty-seven-year-old independent insurance agent from Santa Barbara, California. He just got married for the third time, and he's having a little trouble adjusting to his new life of wedded bliss. "My wife and I just returned from our honeymoon in Hawaii. It was great, and very romantic, too. But she keeps telling me what to do all the time now, much more than she ever did when we were dating. She's always tried to get me to do things, but she used to ask me. Well, I've got news for you, those days are gone. Now she TELLS me what to do. She's even telling me what to say and how to act! I don't understand the sudden change, and to be honest with you, I don't like it very much either."

And this is his third marriage? I'm reminded of Einstein who said the definition of insanity is doing the same thing over and over again but expecting different results. Apparently Don doesn't understand the single most important dynamic when it comes to men and women choosing their mates. A man marries a woman based on who he thinks she is, but a woman marries a man based on who she thinks she can *change* him to become.

Don may want to sign up for the remedial course in Marriage 101, because clearly he can use the help. Not only are men simple beings, but they also tend to exist in the here and now more than there and then, or anywhere else. What they see right in front of them is what they expect they're going to get. Like horses with blinders on, they often miss what goes on in the periphery. That's where they make their first mistake about women. The typical man assumes the woman he sees is the person she's going to be. Poor guy, if only he knew better.

When it comes to seeing what is directly in front of them, men and women tend to operate on two different frequencies. For example, when a guy looks at a kitchen he sees a refrigerator. When a woman looks at a kitchen she sees a four course gourmet meal. He sees what is there, she sees what she believes can be there. The same is true in relationships. When Brad Pitt looked at Angelina Jolie, he saw—well, Angelina Jolie. When Julia Roberts looked at Lyle Lovett, she apparently thought she saw George Clooney!

Women are more holistic, they see beyond the present to what they can have tomorrow. But they also know it will require change in order to get there. The challenge is that guys are reluctant to change, and even if they do, it typically doesn't happen quickly or easily. It's like the very old, but fitting joke: How many psychologists does it take to change a light bulb? The answer is of course only one, but the light bulb has to *really* want to change. So like most guys, Don will simply have to be considered a work in progress.

When it comes to changing men, women tend to fall into one of two camps. Some want men to become the better guys they are capable of being, and others simply want them to stop farting in public and take out the trash. Women in the first camp don't see men as defective and in need of repair. They see them as unique and fascinating beings who left on their own would likely not realize their full potential, and they want to help them achieve it.

The real problem is that as a general rule, men don't want to be changed. They don't want to be sculpted, molded, and shaped into another being. So we have one partner dedicated to bringing about change, with both the insight and foresight to see the benefits that can follow, but the other partner is adamantly unwilling to change. The interpersonal nuances of that pairing bring a whole new meaning to the phrase "politics makes for strange bedfellows."

It might help if men think of living with women as being kind of like having a colonoscopy. They know they don't want to do it, they feel at least a part of their manhood is compromised by doing it, and both the prep work and the procedure are a pain in the ass. But when it's over, they feel better, look better, and are ultimately glad they did it. Don just needs to accept the fact, like millions of men have before him, that he's not the top dog anymore. He should be content being the vice-president of sales and let her be the CEO.

Have I Got a Deal for You!

Getting married, in its simplest form, is a type of sales process. Once the relationship matures past the infatuation stage, it becomes much like shopping for a car, or spending four days and three nights sampling some time-share resort property in the Bahamas. Two people in effect test drive each other to see if they can fit well together as husband and wife. And just as in many sales scenarios, some couples treat each other as prospects while they're dating, but fail to provide the needed customer care after they marry.

Though both genders can be guilty of overselling themselves, since men marry who they see in the present, they expect their bride to continue being the person she is at the moment they marry her.

They don't expect change to occur after the wedding. John Gray, author of *Men Are from Mars, Women Are from Venus*, found that the number one complaint registered by men was that women are always trying to change them. And the number one complaint women made of men was that they don't listen. Could these two charges be related? Maybe the men aren't listening because they don't want to be changed.

Secret No. 23 that men think but don't tell women is, *"Live and let live; don't try to change us."* This one can be hard for women to hear, but if they really want to know what goes on inside the clubhouse, what men really think, this is a big one. Men don't like it when women treat them worse than the Sweathogs from the old *Welcome Back, Kotter* television series. Vinnie Barbarino might have been rather rough around the edges, but the girls were still after him, and "fixing" him wasn't foremost in their minds. Houses are fixer-uppers; men are not.

Justin, thirty-three, an architect from Fort Wayne, Indiana, was married a little over a year ago. He says he went to premarital counseling with his fiancée and still couldn't have seen what was coming. "My wife and I dated for two years before we married. Two years! And during that entire time she was great. She did her thing, I did mine. We did things together. But what she *didn't* do was try to change me. Even when we were engaged and went to premarital counseling together, everything was fine. But after we were married it was suddenly different. She has been correcting me and telling me other ways—what she thinks are better ways—to do things ever since. It's almost like when we were dating, even when we were engaged, she was being the way she thought I wanted her to be. But after the wedding, now that we're married, it's like she thinks she's in charge."

Henry, forty-nine, a construction foreman from Houston, Texas, has been divorced for almost three years. He has tried to develop a few relationships, but has retreated from each one because he says the women were trying to sculpt him into a different man. "I was married to my first wife for twenty years. I've dated my fair share of women over the past few years, but none of them have lasted very long. It's seems so different than when my ex-wife and I were dating. Women don't take a back seat to men anymore, and I guess that's just the way it is. But for me, when they start trying to teach me how to be a different guy or flat out tell me the way I ought to be, that's when I take a hike. I don't need that. I don't try to change them; I let them live the way they choose to live. I just wish women would do the same for me."

Tires and dirty underwear need changing. Men do not. Okay, some men do, but women aren't perfect either. Women wise to Secret No. 23 understand the concept of live and let live. They don't try to change or control men because they are keenly aware that men resist both. And though they know that some men, probably most men, could use some refining, they go about it with subtlety and grace, not with a tire iron.

Other women wonder why they can't keep men around. In focus group after focus group, I heard the same two complaints from women. They can't get a man or they're miffed about why they can't keep the ones they think they might be able to get. And while some just want to play the field, most said they want to meet the kind of guy with whom they can date exclusively, develop a lasting relationship, and eventually marry.

When it comes to guys, serial daters should never be confused with serial monogamists. The former are like an Indian summer— they hang around longer than expected, and the women are always glad they do. The latter are like reflected images in a crystal clear pool of water. They're in it for the long haul until one attempts to change them, and then they disappear. Smart women know men stick around when they can live and let live. Other women keep wondering why they left.

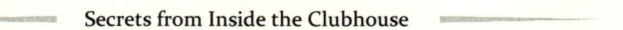

26

A *WOMAN'S* HOME IS HER CASTLE?

Secret No. 24: "Take it easy . . . we don't work for you."

Women have finally learned to follow the golden rule: she who has the gold makes the rules. In the United States today, women are the primary financial decision-makers in more than 50 percent of households, and that statistic jumps to 96 percent if the woman of the house is also a mother. Joint decision-making is customary in approximately 40 percent of the remaining households, so it is estimated that the "man of the house" or "wait until your father gets home" decision-making style so prevalent in the sixties occurs in less than 10 percent of households today.

Now Women Are Head of the Household?

Don should not be surprised that his domicile is not one of them. He should probably be smart and take advantage of it. With some exceptions, women will dress men better than the men dress themselves, feed them better than they eat on their own, help them spend their money more judiciously, and most importantly, find their missing socks so they can make it to their dinner meetings on time.

But while women are becoming the head of the household, a lot of men say they're feeling more like employees and less like husbands. Gary, forty-seven, a married sales manager from Jacksonville, Florida, says his life changed dramatically after he married Lisa. "Frankly,

I'm still in shock, and it's been almost two years since Lisa and I got married. I knew she was a woman who likes to take charge when she's involved in something, but I had no idea she would try to run every aspect of my life. It's like she thinks she's my boss. I have to go to bed at night when she goes to bed, and watch what she wants to watch on television. She questions just about everything I wear, who I'm going to hang with, and what time I'll be home. And if I tell her I'm going to be late, she tells me that if I know what's good for me, I'd better be home by midnight. The other night I got so frustrated I finally shouted at her, 'Take it easy. I don't work for you!'"

Guys approach the altar anticipating that life after the vows have been spoken will be much like it was before they uttered those fateful words, "I do." By contrast, women see the bigger picture, the way things can be better in the future. And now that they're bound by a legal contract as well as an emotional one, they take their job seriously and start down the road to getting there as soon as possible.

Guys see what they like, think *logically* in the here and now, and thus see no reason to change. Girls see what they like, think *relationally* into the future, and thus see valid reasons to change. So while guys fear that they may have married somebody other than who they thought their bride is, girls are content knowing that the reclamation project is finally underway.

They Can't Help It; It's in Their Blood

"It's hard to kiss the lips at night that chewed your ass out all day long." These are actual words from a country-music video being passed around on the Internet. Guys can really identify with the tune. Some men feel they've been corrected more times than Willie Nelson's tax return. Are guys really that inept? Maybe some women as new heads of the household feel it necessary to mark their territory, to plant their branding irons firmly into the backside of their new steers. Or is it that women just can't help themselves? Maybe it's in their blood.

A lot of men are uttering under their breath that old cliché, "Who died and made her the boss?" At the offices of Our Life Together, Inc., here is a short list of some of the injunctions and maxims men report women have been hurling at them. Some of them might sound familiar.

- "Don't read the paper when you're sitting on the couch; you'll get newsprint on the leather!"
- "Don't throw your sweat-soaked workout stuff in the laundry basket; hang it up to dry out first!"
- "Don't park your car so close to mine in the garage!"
- "Don't put the dishes in the dishwasher until you at least rinse them first!"
- "Don't stay in the shower too long; you'll run up the water bill!"
- "Don't tell the neighbors I never help with the yard work!"
- "Don't drive the car like a maniac, and stop pressing on the gas so much!"
- "Don't set the temperature so low; I'm freezing in here!"
- "Don't turn on that damn football game now— I'm trying to watch fifty-year-old reruns of *The Golden Girls.*
- "Don't come in the house with that stuff on your shoes; you'll track it all over the carpet!"
- "Don't give me that crap. I know you were out with Bob, so I know what you were *really* doing!"
- "For Chrissakes, can't you at least courtesy flush? Light a match in there, and make sure you spray the Renuzit before you come out!"

Truth be told, most guys could use some remedial help with toilet training. Maybe the women who issued these injunctions have exhausted other, more amenable ways of asking for some cooperation and help around the house first, and found themselves left with no alternative but to fire such salvos as a last resort. But come on, ladies, *The Golden Girls* over a football game?

But of all the rules and regulations, the reprimands and restrictions, the mandates and maxims girls can launch at their guys, there are two others in particular that stand out so vibrantly they deserve special mention, one at a time. First, the infamous, "You're not going out looking like *that*, are you?"

I have some firsthand experience with this one. I was getting ready to play golf with a few friends one day. On a golf course in Texas in the summer, in humid, one-hundred-ten-degree heat, you sweat more than Kobe Bryant at a paternity hearing. Guys are less concerned with how fashionably they dress, and more with keeping hydrated and not looking like poster children for melanoma. My wife stopped me as I was about to leave, snickered, gave me that what-a-stupid-idiot-you-are look, and issued the command for me to change clothes.

"You can't wear those shorts with that shirt!"

"Why not? They're khakis, aren't they?"

"No," she scolded. "They're an *off-green* khaki. You can't wear off-green khakis with a brown, patterned shirt. It looks ridiculous!"

"But look, babe, it's got little blue diamonds all over it."

"Exactly," she quips back. "That's my point. It doesn't match. You won't look good, and you'll embarrass yourself in front of your friends."

"But my friends couldn't care less what I wear. They won't even notice! Hell, Jackson usually wears cargo shorts and a T-shirt."

"I don't care what *he* wears; he's a Neanderthal anyway. And whether *they* notice or not, others will. Now hurry up and change before you leave, or you're going to be late. And don't forget to pick up some skim milk at the grocery store on your way back home; I want it for my cereal in the morning."

I wanted to come home later to a house sans any land mines, so I changed, passed inspection, and thanked her for her valuable input. I know better than to try to explain that my tee-to-green fashion sense will have absolutely no affect on my friends or anyone else on the course. Instead I took a deep breath, zipped my lip, got in the car, and left, content in knowing that while I was on the golf course sweating my butt off, I'd at least be doing it in a pair of shorts and a shirt that matched. We divorced a year later.

And then there's the most infamous of all injunctions, the one every guy has heard as he crawls into bed with visions of sugar dancing in his head. The one command that knows no language barrier, is universal in its usage and relevance, and is the one guys least want to hear. It also needs no explanation or supporting evidence: "Don't do that to me *now*; I'm trying to sleep!"

Secret No. 24 that men think but don't tell women is, *"Take it easy . . . we don't work for you."* No matter the changing times and shifting of responsibilities, guys aren't *employed* by women. In a country where the divorce rate is better than 50 percent, slightly more than one out of every two marriages fail, and it could be at least in part because men really do feel shackled by the proverbial ball and chain. Do men just need to get with the program? Maybe it's time for Martha Stewart's *Living* magazine to feature The Good Husband's Guide on how to be the perfect husband.

A significant number of the married men I interviewed insist their wives are running things at home. From the color of the carpets and the paint on the walls, to the settings for the thermostats and the furniture for the kids' rooms, women are the real decision-makers. A lot of men even said they give their paychecks to their wives each payday and have to ask for a few shekels per week so they'll have some walking-around money. Ah yes, the golden rule in its most shimmering essence.

Bert, thirty-two, a broker for a food company from Columbia, South Carolina, thinks he should be punching a clock at home. "I love my wife, but I'm wearing real thin with her acting like she's the boss all the time. It's like she never stops thinking about what needs to be done or what she wants done. And most of the time she wants me to do it. I wouldn't mind so much if I felt like we were equal partners, but most of the time I feel like an hourly worker who never gets to punch out. And I never get paid overtime either."

Josh, thirty-seven, an airline pilot from Southlake, Texas, shares his perspective. "For me it was like she saw the way I lived, but never really said anything about it until after we were married. Then it was like she just took over. I mean, she's got me doing stuff around the house I never even thought of doing. I wish we could have talked about this stuff before we got married. Sometimes I feel like she actually thinks I work for her."

Al, a forty-nine-year-old banker from Tulsa, Oklahoma, says his wife acts like his boss and he thinks he's figured out why. "I think my wife knows that even if there are a lot of things to talk about, she can't count on me to keep the conversation going, so the only things she ends up saying are the orders she gives me. Otherwise there probably wouldn't be a whole lot of other communication at all."

Jason, forty-five, a retailer from St. Paul, Minnesota, says he wishes women would think about how they communicate with men. "I assume my wife means well when she gives me her honey-do list, but I sure wish she'd show me a little more respect. Sometimes I really feel like she thinks I'm her servant and that she's in charge and has the right to tell me what to do. Just once I'd like her to ask me to do something nicely. There's a difference between doing something because I want to versus because I'm being told I have no choice."

If that old cliché is true, that a man's home is his castle, in the new millennium his manhood seems to have somehow found its way into the moat. Have men done such a bad job managing the homestead that they need to be fired and replaced? Why are more and more women taking command around the house? Maybe the more accurate question to ask is, why not? It might just be time we start saying a *woman's* home is her castle.

When it comes to running the household, women may be able to do a better job. They certainly are much better at multitasking than men. For example, most women have no problem picking up the dry cleaning, basting a turkey, preparing a Grand Marnier soufflé, changing the baby's diaper, running in a 5K race to benefit breast-cancer patients, shaving their legs, pressing their husbands' slacks and finding his missing Polo shirt, all while simultaneously creating a fifty-column spreadsheet on the computer for a project at work. And wait until you see what they can do *after* lunch! Maybe if the job fits, they should wear it.

Evidence exists to support the claim that the balance of power has indeed shifted. Certain behavioral changes in men suggest they've become not only subservient to women, but worse, fearful of them. A lot of guys are running scared and saying things like, "My wife will kill me if I do that!" Or, "Don't tell my girlfriend about this!" Or, "I've got to check with my wife first." And, "Oh hell, she'd never let me do *that*!"

One guy said he enjoys a couple of drinks at happy hour, then bolts home chewing an entire pack of gum along the way to kill the smell of the alcohol on his breath. He wants his wife to think he's just coming home from work. Why the cowardice? Are men afraid they can't have good relationships with women unless they relinquish total control to them? Guys waxing their balls may be in style in metrosexual America, but just like wearing white shoes with pair of plaid sans-a-belt slacks, castration is absolutely out of the question.

Wait a Minute. Could Men Be Smarter Than They Look?

Maybe the guys have figured out that they no longer want to be in charge. Maybe they've learned how to play the game and just aren't admitting it. While they may appear to have given up and conceded victory, their undaunted compliance could be masking a clandestine, more sophisticated modus operandi they've been executing flawlessly for years, and it's been getting them the very results they seek. If indeed we tend to become what we think about most, maybe guys have seen the inherent benefit in being simpletons. *Cogito, ergo sum!*

You've no doubt heard the phrase, "Dumb like a fox." Men could be smarter than women think. Most of them, knowing that women will fire off the mandates and corrections anyway, may have inoculated themselves with highly practiced rhetoric such as, "I didn't hear that," or, "I don't understand," and "She'll forget she said it, anyway" as coping mechanisms. And they can always feign the, "I can't hear you. You're breaking up. I'll call you back later," when they're on their cell phone. Men may actually be smarter than they look.

Women who really "get it" when it comes to Secret No. 24 know that when a woman tells a man to do something, she means it more as a utilitarian efficiency and less as a Draconian command. She also knows better than to order her man about, instead choosing to ask for his help rather than demand it. She knows he doesn't work for her. She also knows there is a way to get him to work *with* her. Ultimately, she's not out to control or change him. She's just trying to make sure the mother ship is running smoothly so that the Fourth of

July barbecue she has choreographed for thirty people comes off without a hitch.

There's a New Sheriff in Town

But if more women are heading up households, does that mean there's a new sheriff in town? What are guys supposed to do now? Most men are ill equipped to be deputies. Were this the twenty-first century remake of *The Andy Griffith Show*, there would be a million Barney Fifes out there running in circles with one foot nailed to the ground. Expecting a man to live up to a woman's standards is probably as unrealistic as expecting a woman to live down to a man's.

Is a man's home *really* no longer his castle? If women have become the financial decision-makers and control the day-to-day operations of the household, maybe men need to be demoted. But what about the economic power in the relationship? Some say breadwinner status should equate to head of household. Since women are the financial decision-makers in 96 percent of the households with children, maybe more of them should also be earning enough scratch to qualify as the primary breadwinners.

Women really could be the CEO of Our Life Together, Inc., and men really could work for them. It might not be all that bad for the guys. At the very least they could put in a request for some overtime pay and utilize the occasional sick day when necessary. Of course, they could no longer say, "Take it easy. I don't work for you." And every man would need to remember that his woman would be able to bring home the bacon, fry it up in the pan, and whenever she feels the need, always help him remember she can forget he's her man!

27

¿Cómo Se Dice la Jefa en Inglés?

Secret No. 25: "Speak English; we don't understand womaneze."

"Be honest with me," "We need to talk," and "I want a baby." Three four-word phrases that make men run faster than Forrest Gump hightailing away from a Mensa meeting. Most men are not bilingual. They don't speak womaneze. They can't interpret the female code, and deductive reasoning isn't their best asset.

While men are more direct when they speak, women tend to speak indirectly. More important, women often expect the men in their lives to understand, decode, and follow their indirect speech. The problem this poses for most guys is that they don't have the cerebral bandwidth to pick up on it. They just want to know who won the Lakers game.

When men and women do speak to each other, it is often like two people tossing water balloons. Each one tries to duck away from what he doesn't want and catch what she does want, while knowing that they'll probably get wet in the process. Classes in womaneze might help. But since men are much more in tune with Dr. Seuss than Dr. Phil, simplification works much better than therapeutic intervention. Enough with the pedantry, ladies—just say it!

As a favor to men everywhere, below are the interpretations of fifteen typical womaneze phrases guys hear routinely. On the left is the encoding of the message being sent (what the women say), and on the right the decoding of that message so men can fully understand what women really mean.

Secrets from Inside the Clubhouse

When a woman says . . .	She really means . . .
Would you like to go to the movies?	I want to go to the movies!
I'd like you to take out the trash.	Take out the trash now!
Call me.	Call me within an hour.
Please call me.	Call me every day.
Fine!	Shut the hell up!
I'll be ready in a minute.	Sit down, have a drink, watch TV. I'm getting ready, and I'm on "female time."
I'm starving!	Oh, I'll just have a salad.
I'm fat.	Tell me you think I have a good body.
Oh, him? He's an obnoxious pig!	If I were single, I'd have sex with him.
I really want to wear pants tonight.	I don't want to shave my legs.
Do you think my friend Michelle is pretty?	You'd better not have an answer for that one. And if you do, it better be to tell me I'm prettier than she is.
We can't afford this house we're living in.	I want you to take me on a vacation.
Do you think I can wear a thong bathing suit?	I can't wait to wear my new thong bathing suit next week when I go to Cancun on my girls-only trip.
Hey, good lookin', buy me a drink?	I don't want you; I just want a free drink.
Not tonight, honey, I have a headache.	I'm not in the mood, but if I change my mind, I'll take care of it myself.

After I showed this list to a group of married men, all of whom perceive themselves as ranking lower than their wives on the Our Life Together, Inc., organizational chart, they slapped themselves on the forehead a few times and sought refuge down the hall in another focus group debating boxers or briefs.

At least men, being the simpletons they are, speak in a language easy to understand. For example, when a man says, "Honey, you're losing by three, there are two down in the bottom of the ninth, nobody on base, and you're looking at a 0-2 count," everybody knows he really means, "I would appreciate it if you would ask me first before telling your mother that I'll be glad to go shopping with her." Simplicity is the spice of life.

Communicating one another's needs is a critical factor in any successful union, be it in a marriage, a romantic relationship, or even between co-workers. Men and women must be able to articulate what they want from each other in a language both can understand. There must be a sender of the message and a receiver to complete the transmission. Men have little problem being the sender of messages, but they tend to be lazy receivers and miss what women are trying to say. Somehow a lot gets lost in translation. Though men don't understand womaneze, women still have to be heard.

Women Have Needs, Too

Women are genetically predisposed, indeed *driven*, to satisfy four key needs. Once they successfully handle the life-sustaining requirements of food, clothing, and shelter, they seek to satisfy their needs for Verbal Intimacy, Sexual Intimacy, Shopping, and of course, Travel. To women, these essential needs serve as primary motivators for a well-balanced life. What a shame they seem so opaque to most men.

Just as men claim sex, work, money, and war are indicators by which they define their manhood, women feel compelled to satisfy their four primary needs in order to achieve and maintain homeostasis. They *need* to talk, they *need* to have sex, they *need* to shop, and they can do all three when they travel. Most men can satisfy only two of the four, only some of the time, and typically not more than one at a time. They don't speak womaneze, they can't really appreciate the value of an adequate wardrobe, and they've burned up their frequent flyer miles.

But women are nothing if not resilient and resourceful. They are driven to converse, to talk with others, so they utilize their best friends for that. They have sexual needs to be satisfied, and though they might prefer a man to help with those, some of the more progressive ladies keep at least one reliable alternative in the nightstand if necessary. They are driven to take flight on the sojourns of their choice, and they have a number of qualified companions willing to vacation with them in the wine country, the Bahamas, Cancun, or wherever their wanderlust takes them. They are also driven to shop, and they all know the malls open daily at ten.

Secret No. 25 that men think but don't tell women is, *"Speak English—we don't understand womaneze."* Again, men are literal beings. When a woman says, "We need to talk," a man doesn't know what she means. He immediately thinks logically, linearly, and exercises his critical thinking skills. He wonders to himself, "Talk about what? Who goes first? Why is this important?" And most critically, "How long will this take?"

Mark, a thirty-seven year old accountant from Durango, Colorado, thinks men could be more attentive to women's needs if they spoke a language guys could understand. "I know my wife likes to talk. But I'm really not much of a talker. If she would speak English and not whatever that stuff she says is, I would better understand what she needs or wants from me and give it to her. The other day she asked me if I would be available to help her sort through some junk in the attic. I asked her when did she want to do it, and she said probably Friday after work. Well, this was Tuesday so I didn't worry about it. Plus, she said *probably* not *definitely* so I figured she'd tell me later in the week if we were definitely going to do it. I never heard about it again. Then, I come home on Friday and she's up in the attic sorting through the stuff, pissed off at me for not helping."

Robert, forty-three, a contractor from Mesa, Arizona, says if a woman would be more direct, more specific, her man would be more willing to engage. "I hate it when my wife just says we need to talk. I never know what it's about or what I'm supposed to say, and it seems as if it happens most when I'm about to leave for work or to go play golf with my buddies. I wish she would just say something more direct like, 'When you get back, can we spend a few minutes talking about what we want to get Anne and Jim for a wedding present?' At least I would know the subject, how long it will take, and how to be prepared. I wish I didn't have to second guess her all of the time."

Harry, forty, a shipping clerk from Anchorage, Alaska, says he wishes his girlfriend would better clarify what she wants when she sends him out on an errand. "Picking up stuff a woman wants from the grocery store can be a hazard to your health. If she needs me to pick up more than two items, she should give me a written list and include the brand name, size, and whatever else is important. Otherwise I will likely come home with a quart of whole milk when she specifically wanted a gallon of skim and forgotten all about the laundry detergent and facial soap. I've got other, more important things on my mind."

Women wise to Secret No. 25 know that vague communication with men just doesn't work. They realize that guys are both simple and literal, and they refrain from using womaneze when speaking to them. Since they know men are not bilingual, they speak this special, esoteric language only when their girlfriends are over and they don't want the men to have a clue about what they're saying.

Smart women know to communicate in terms men can understand. For example, if a woman wants her man to go to the grocery store, a place most men avoid like a rectal exam, she says, "Please pick up one gallon of Oak Farms 2-percent milk with vitamins A and D, a box of Wheat Thins–Low Sodium, and the latest issue of *Maxim* magazine." The first two items require specific directions and are really the only things she needs. The last one is just an incentive to get him to go to the store. It works every time.

If she wants to go to Jamaica on vacation with her girlfriends, she says, "Suzanne, Lori, Cindy, and I want to go to Jamaica July 24–28. I would love for you to go with us. It will be a lot of fun. We'll get facials, enjoy massages, and sip umbrella drinks on the beach all day. What do you think?" He'll wish them a safe trip, call three or four of his buddies, and begin planning for the time off.

Being direct with men is the most effective way to communicate. Stating specific places, people, dates, and activities helps guys better understand what women are saying. They simply aren't smart enough to decipher womaneze. They may know what reading an audible is, or the precise time for the linebackers to blitz, but grasping the more subjective nuances of the much more sophisticated language of women is simply a meta-cognitive process that exceeds their normal range of capabilities.

Dogs have to be specifically told to sit, stay, or heel. Maybe that explains why they are man's best friend.

Feminine Privilege

What? No thank-you? YOU'RE WELCOME, anyway! JERK!
What a "Y-chromosome" cliché. JERK!

28

Yesterday All Our Troubles Seemed So Far Away

Some women just can't get enough . . . not that! . . . I mean *secrets*! This book has been about how much women's roles have changed since the feminist movement of the late sixties. Each chapter shared one secret that men think but don't tell women. In this highly classified special section, Chapter 28 shares not one, but *five* more secrets men think about and tell each other but would never tell a woman directly. Mental morsels about common courtesy, time of arrival for a date, attraction, shopping, and privilege—inside information women won't want to miss. This chapter is like a bonus. It's like when famed marketer Ron Popiel barks in his infomercials for the Ronco pocket fisherman, the famous food dehydrator, or the infamous cans of spray-on hair, "But wait! There's more!! Have your credit card ready. Operators are standing by NOW! Take advantage of this fabulous opportunity; you'll be glad you did!

Common Courtesy

"Please" and "Thank you." "Yes Ma'am" and "No Sir." Common courtesies used every day. Or are they? Long ago and far away, in a land that time forgot, men bowed as they took the delicate hand of a woman and lightly kissed it as a showing of great respect. Today such behavior is scoffed at and labeled condescending or sexist. Once upon a time men could also be seen opening doors for women. And in those days, the women typically said, "Thank you."

But just like watching *Seinfeld*, today such pleasantries can be seen only in reruns.

Secret No. 26 that men think but don't tell women is, *"It's okay to say 'Thank you' when we open a door for you."* Will, forty-three, a consultant from Aliso Viejo, California, is tired of feeling invisible.

"I can remember a time when women appreciated men opening doors for them. And men wanted to do it. *I* wanted to do it, and I still do. That's just how I was raised. But nowadays I often feel like I don't exist. The other day I stepped up, opened a door for a woman, and she just walked right through without a word. I stood there dumbfounded for a moment, then said 'You're welcome!' as she walked away. She didn't even acknowledge me. I'm getting real tired of the lack of common courtesies being demonstrated by women. Sometimes I even feel like I'm just a hood ornament to my wife."

Women. You can't live with them, and maybe it's time men learned to live without them. It shouldn't matter what gender a person is; anybody who has the courtesy to open a door for another should be thanked. But I have to jump in here on this one. I have experienced exactly what Will describes many times. I too have opened doors for women, and they've walked right past me without even the slightest gesture of thanks. It didn't used to be that way.

Do we blame such simple atrocities on the feminists? They were the ones who worked tirelessly to orient women to hate men or at the very least disrespect them. Or should we blame the parents? Common courtesies should be part and parcel of human interpersonal relations, regardless of gender, and should first be taught and modeled at home. Maybe these particular women weren't encouraged to give thanks when someone does something nice for them.

Women wise to Secret No. 26 are mature and secure enough within themselves to offer a simple thank-you when men open doors for them. They also are happy to do the same for men without compromising their femininity. And when they do, they too appreciate being thanked.

It's a travesty this secret among men is uttered at all. It's a new millennium. Women can do anything men can do. Maybe they should open their own doors and forget about the common courtesies of everyday life. Maybe it's also time we call manhole covers *personhole* covers.

Time of Arrival

Most people are familiar with what ETA stands for: Estimated Time of Arrival. In dating behavior, this would mean the time the girl will be ready for the guy to arrive at her place to pick her up for the date. Sure, and every now and then even a blind squirrel finds a nut.

Every guy knows that if he is due to pick his date up at seven o'clock, she'll be ready to go around seven-thirty, if he's lucky. Just like dancing, inordinate primping is simply something girls are born to do. Guys would much rather be told the Estimated Time of Departure, the ETD, the actual time she'll be ready to leave. With that valuable bit of information, they could take advantage of the extra time to watch *Sports Center* on ESPN, read a novel, or rebuild the transmission in their Corvettes before ringing her doorbell.

Secret No. 27 that men think but don't tell women is, *"Don't give us an ETA . . . give us an ETD."* Christopher, a forty-one-year-old computer programmer from Dunbar, Pennsylvania, really wishes women would be more realistic with their time management.

"I never mind having to wait for a few minutes if my date isn't ready to go when I get to her place, but if she's going to be thirty minutes, why can't she just tell me to come at about the time she'll be ready? Especially if it's the first time I'm at her place. I sit around with nothing to do, and I don't feel comfortable just flipping on her TV unless she offers it first. And when a girl has a dog, it can really be a hassle. One girl had a Jack

Russell terrier. Those damn dogs must be on speed. He jumped all over me and shed like crazy. I had to take my clothes to the dry cleaners the next day. I wish we could have ETDs instead of ETAs."

ETDs would certainly save time and could cut down on the dry cleaning bills too. But just as it's in vogue to be socially late to dinner parties, maybe women just want to savor the opportunity to make a grand entrance. Maybe it's called estimated time of arrival because it isn't an exact science. Still, no doubt Christopher would prefer an alternative warm-up act and preferably one without four legs and fur.

Women wise to Secret No. 27 realize that guys tend to monitor time by following sidereal order, focusing on a fixed reference within a quantifiable, mechanistic means of measurement. In other words, they use a clock. What a novel concept. And being the literal fellows they are, if a woman tells them to pick her up at eight, they look at the clock and then show up at eight.

Smart women know men can't translate the numerical equivalent of time on the clock, in this case the big hand on the twelve and the little hand on the eight, into understanding that eight really means three wardrobe changes south of the hour. Resourceful ladies adjust accordingly by having a beer, a dozen bite-sized pizzas from Sam's Club fresh out of the oven, and a note taped to the remote that says, "Help yourself, I'll be out soon." Guys will wait for *these* girls until the next vernal equinox.

Attraction

Some women make fantastic jackhammer operators. Others make great girlfriends and wives. Guys may talk a good game, but at the end of the day, they'll take Suzy with a spreadsheet over Rosie with a riveter every time. Most men still believe male means masculine and female means feminine. Men are supposed to be macho, and women are supposed to be, well, womanly.

Secret No. 28 that men think but don't tell women is, *"We'll drink with Serena Williams, but we'll marry Jennifer Aniston."* There are exceptions to most every sociological convention in life. But most men want the women they date and marry to be smaller than them, physically weaker than them, and more feminine than them. Guys will have a drink with most any girl, but when it comes to dating or marriage, while it's okay for women to be intelligent and powerful, men prefer women who use tools of their trade made by Microsoft, not by Craftsman.

Brandon, forty-seven, an analyst from St. Louis, Missouri, says he appreciates progressive women, but still wants them to be mostly traditional in both size and deportment. "I like seeing women rise to the top in business and sports and in other aspects of life, too. And I love watching them play, tennis especially. Some of them are just stunning to look at. But when I find out that they're six feet tall, or that they are as strong as an ox and weigh nearly as much as I do, it just turns me off. Though I love watching them compete, I wouldn't want to date any of them. I really want to date only truly feminine women."

Serena Williams is a beautiful woman. She may be feminine, too. But she is also built like a middle linebacker. To a lot of men, she's just not feminine enough. By contrast, Jennifer Aniston is equally successful in her chosen profession, but she has retained both the physical characteristics and the femininity that really turn men on. Both women have arrived at a point in their careers where they are accomplished, appreciated, and powerful. They've each made a bundle of dough too. But if given the choice, most men would pick Jennifer over Serena.

Women wise to Secret No. 28 know that men still appreciate traditional femininity and give it to them. They understand that just as they want men to be masculine, not too in touch with their feminine side, men want them to be feminine. Serena Williams is an accomplished athlete and may be very sweet, too. But she's never been called America's Sweetheart.

Face it, guys still want the girl next door, unless of course, she's six-foot-four.

Shopping

Retail therapy. Every woman knows that phrase; every man wishes she didn't. Shopping is therapeutic to women just like *not* shopping is to men. Men like to spend time in the women's clothing section at Neiman's about as much as women want to tool around in the hardware store. But shopping really isn't a problem for men until women want them to tag along. Trapped for hours between two clearance racks, most men aren't resourceful enough to do much more than count their arteries. That's when they need EGT, Elective Gastronomical Therapy.

Secret No. 29 that men think but don't tell women is, *"No trip to the mall is complete without a pretzel."* Tom, thirty-nine, an advertising sales executive from Green Bay, Wisconsin, says the only redeeming value he sees in going shopping with his girlfriend is his customary stop at the pretzel shop.

"My girlfriend loves to go shopping. I enjoy it about as much as I do a root canal. But I know I've got to put in a little time walking the mall with her every now and then to keep the peace. But what I find helps me is that I can tell her that while she's browsing the racks I'm going to get a pretzel and I'll be back shortly. It works every time. I can be gone for thirty minutes, and when I get back, I can tell her I ran in to a couple of friends or I would have been back sooner. Then I compliment her on how good she looks in the dress she's trying on, and I'm good to go."

At the mall, most men prefer pretzels to panties. They just don't possess the cerebral bandwidth to watch as their other half sorts through garment after garment, trying on a dozen or so, only to then put them all back, thank the sales clerk, and head for the next boutique.

Women wise to Secret No. 29 understand that to most guys *shopping* means a quick trip to the corner convenience store for some chips, dip, and a twelve pack. Trapped in a trendy boutique, most of them feel more out of place than a Rastafarian at an after-five dinner party at Lord Buckingham's. Smart women know if they're going to take their guys with them when they go out for some retail therapy, they make sure it's to a mall where their wayward delinquents can wander about aimlessly and where no trip is complete without a pretzel.

A Woman's-Eye View

Remember Mort Sahl? When the well-known comedian and social commentator in the sixties and seventies was asked by a talk show host what he thought about the women's liberation movement, he replied, "I don't understand why women want equal rights. Why would they want to lower themselves?"

Good men have always put women on a figurative pedestal. They were taught both to respect women as the softer, more fragile of the sexes and to honor them for their potency and ability to create life. Indeed, most women had a pretty good deal going until Betty Friedan claimed all sex within a marriage was rape and that women were trapped in a state of domestic indentured servitude. Women started focusing their woman's-eye view on what was going on below them and decided the penthouse and pampering they were enjoying was not the ultimate gig in town.

Secret No. 30 that men think but don't tell women is, *"Don't resist the pedestal . . . just enjoy the view."* Women have greater opportunities than ever, but men like Lou, forty-seven, a pediatrician from Dallas, Texas, think they don't realize it.

"I know most women think it's still a man's world. But for the most part, women have it made. They can get educated and have careers, earn good money, and still be pampered by guys. And most of the time, the guys still pay for everything too, even though they know women have their own money. The truth is, most men really do put women up on a pedestal. What's strange to me is why women don't just enjoy it up there instead of constantly trying to come down here and mingle about with us."

Smart women know how to use Secret No. 30 to their advantage. They understand they are living in a time of unprecedented prosperity and opportunity for women. But they also know that men still want to be chivalrous knights in shining armor, and they don't discourage them. These women let men put them on a pedestal because they know it's a privileged position, and the women who complain about it likely do so precisely because they don't have it.

Wise women like the view from the top. They enjoy the perks that come with the job, and know it's real nice work if they can get it. Plus, it provides the perfect vantage point from which to keep an eye on the men working diligently to ascend to the apex of their perch for a mere moment with her royal highness. They also content themselves with the knowledge that they can fly away at a moment's notice and return when the coast is clear. Alas, mere crumbs for the peasants. It's good to be the queen.

IT'S A REAL, REAL, REAL, REAL WORLD

As they left the night club, John and Dan had second thoughts about who had actually "picked up" whom.

29

HAVE WOMEN BECOME THE SUPERIOR SEX?

When interacting with women, many men these days are more uncomfortable than a towel boy at a lesbian spa resort. They don't know the rules, the roles, or what constitutes proper etiquette. Many of them feel inadequate, that they have lost some of their potency as men, and they don't understand how to relate to women anymore. They're tired of being made to feel like everything bad that's ever happened to women is their fault, and some men say at times they actually feel they have to apologize for being born male.

Sam, thirty-five, a financial advisor from Houston, Texas, says he's lived all of this firsthand. "If I hear one more woman tell me how oppressed women have been by men, I swear I'll duct tape her mouth shut. I'm really tired of being told how unfair everything is for them and how men are constantly taking advantage of women. It may have been that way for a long time, but it's not that way anymore. I'm not the one who did those things. That all happened before my time. I just wish women would stop blaming us."

Gene, a fifty-one-year-old driver for UPS from Harrisburg, Pennsylvania, says women have not only beaten up on him, but they're also targeting men in general. "It seems like a lot of women have jumped on the bandwagon, like it's now fashionable to dish on men for just about any reason. They complain about men in the workplace, how they are at home, how little they understand women, and how they don't take care of women like they should. Excuse me? Half of the time they're beating us up for not letting them take care of *us*!

Sometimes I actually wish I could go through one week without ever even seeing a woman!"

Many men feel they are expected to be at once powerful yet tender, persuasive yet vulnerable, unyielding yet emotional. Is that realistic? Do we want men to wear a jock and a bra at the same time? Carve up the turkey and cut up the quiche? Go away, a little closer, then hurry up and wait? They feel they're being asked to be all things to all people at all times, and all while getting pushed to the back of the line and expected not to complain about it.

Rick, thirty-five, a massage therapist from Key Largo, Florida, hears about this double standard all the time. "I perform massage therapy on about thirty clients a week, and most of them are women. When they're laying there talking to me, some of them just rip men apart. I guess they don't put me in the same category as other men, I don't know, maybe because of my job. But they can be so critical and yet talk out of two sides of their mouths. One minute they're saying men are pigs with no feelings or emotions, and the next minute they say too many men have softened up and they need to man up and take charge. I don't think these women really know what they want."

Rick's words may be more on the mark than people think. It seems there are just as many women as men confused by the upending of long-established gender roles. For hundreds, even thousands of years, men and women each had a playbook of sorts, accepted conventions and maxims that enabled them to coexist and share the planet peacefully, most of the time.

Men understood what it meant to be men, and women were clear about how to be women. What I found most surprising from my interviews and research was that women also say they no longer understand the rules and roles. Both men and women told me they just want to get along and quell the constant push-pull sense of antagonism so prevalent between the sexes these days.

A lot of women are trying to enjoy the advantages they have now that their mothers didn't have, such as college educations, career positions, their own money, and their own homes. But they still want to be treated like ladies, pampered and catered to by men. Meanwhile, a lot of men believe women are blatantly taking advantage of them, operating from a sense of entitlement, enjoying the best of both worlds whether the men like it or not. Sam thinks women are trying to take over.

"I think women are trying to rule over men. Now that they have all the opportunities men have, they're going too far with it and they're practicing a double standard. It's not enough for them to be in the workplace with us. No, they have to keep talking about those million cracks in the glass ceiling as though it's their God-given right to be on the top and in charge. Meanwhile, they still want us to pay for everything and do the heavy lifting around the house. They act like they're the brains and we're just the brawn."

Have women stormed the castle in a concerted effort to overthrow the patriarchy and put themselves in charge? Maybe it is less an uprising than a long-overdue balancing act on the slippery tightrope of life. Women are simply coming into their own, finding their rightful place in a world controlled by men for too long. Men just need time to understand better and adjust to what appears to be inevitable and justifiable change.

But, are women really the superior sex? Record numbers of femes sole keep reminding us they don't need men anymore, so maybe it's true. Consider some of the evidence. There are already more women in the U.S. workforce than men, and more women than men are enrolled in college. Women are ascending to the highest levels in both government and corporate America, and they're having babies without a male partner in their lives.

Women tend to be better at multitasking, their hearing is more acute, they typically have better verbal ability, and they can see the world from a more holistic, global perspective than men. They're also the only gender that can get pregnant and create new human beings inside their bodies, save maybe that one guy who made the news as a medical anomaly. Plus, women can walk and chew gum at the same time, and we've already said they have memories like a steel trap! All that, and they can have multiple orgasms too? Is it even a fair question?

What's Up with This Metrosexual Thing?

American society has sexual identity issues. Androgyny is being mass marketed, replete with specialty shops whose entire inventory consists of unisex fashion. Women are wearing suits and ties to the office, sending men flowers, and having their own mortgages. Men are nurses, administrative assistants, and flight attendants. They're using skin bronzers and getting manicures, pedicures, facials, and waxes. Women are wearing Jockey-brand underwear to bed, and men are wearing Lycra leotards to jog in public! Women have short hair and sideburns, men are highlighting and wearing earrings.

At the office, women wear low-cut tops and thigh-high skirts and bend over men's desks to "go over the spreadsheet." Men are expected to treat the exchange exactly as they would had Melvin from accounting dropped by in his sans-a-belt slacks and Hush Puppies or risk being reported to HR. Meanwhile, men are not permitted to dress provocatively at work. They're not allowed to bare their chests or show off their legs. Or are they?

Enter the metrosexual. What exactly does metrosexual mean? Is it some form of sex *in* the city, metro—sexual? Supposedly, it is a term meant to represent the guy who is somewhere between heterosexual and homosexual. So why don't we just call him the middlesexual? How about the intersexual? Or just call him by his actual name: Ryan Seacrest.

He waxes his body hair, shaves his privates and his armpits, gets facials and manicures, and uses moisturizers. He shops at Neiman Marcus, reads *Lucky* magazine, takes cooking classes, and sends holiday cards to his friends. He tears up each week when he watches *Extreme Makeover: Home Edition,* and he TiVos *Queer Eye for the Straight Guy.* In short, the metrosexual male is the heterosexual male officially feminized.

What scares me the most is that some of those guys are starting to look *real* good! They've got better skin and more attractive bikini lines than most women. A lot of them are luxuriating in bubble baths and taking longer than the ladies to get dressed. Are we witnessing, as one man I interviewed suggested, the pussyification of America?

It may be somewhat of a generational thing too. When I ask baby boomer women about metrosexuals, they all but unanimously give me two thumbs down, saying real men should have hair on their chest, under their arms, and in all of the other "right" places. But when I ask my college students, they are adamant that men should have absolutely no hair on their chests and only minimal growth on their legs and arms. Some coeds even voted for none anywhere on their bodies! Ironically, baby boomer women think men should shave their faces every day while the coeds favor a three-day growth. Go figure.

Searching for Proper Protocol

So for men, things are tough all over. If women haven't been the superior sex in the past, they seem to be now. Consider how confusing it can be for men these days. Below is a list of twenty social conundrums they wrestle with daily. When they're not busy waxing their backs or attending sensitivity training, they're pondering how to be a man in an increasingly woman's world. Women can probably identify with a lot of these too. Feel free to add to the list. We'll use the Shakespearian method of inquiry. To be or not to be, that is the question. Whether 'tis nobler:

- To open a door for a woman or not to open it
- To shake a woman's hand firmly or softly
- To offer to pay the check in full or to let her offer to pay
- To split the check or not to split the check
- To drive when we go to the mall or to let her drive
- To call a woman first or not to call but wait to be called
- To offer the first-date goodnight kiss or not to offer it
- To pick her up on a first date or meet her instead if she doesn't know me yet
- To be in touch with her feelings or not be in touch with her feelings
- To be in touch with my feminine side or not be in touch with my feminine side
- To have sex on the first date or not to have sex on the first date, or second, or third
- To initiate sex or let her initiate sex
- To be asked out or not to be asked out by her first
- To pay a woman a compliment about her looks at work or not to pay a compliment because she might call it sexual harassment
- To report being sexually harassed myself or not to report it
- To have a woman for a boss or not to have a woman for a boss
- To compete in sports against a woman or not to compete against her
- To lift weights with a woman or not to lift with her

- To let her run the household or not to let her run it
- To wax or not to wax

Can't We All Just Get Along?

Women and men were not designed to be homogenized. With rare exception, the typical girl no more wants to slip on a Nike sports jock than the typical guy wants to wriggle into a push-up Wonderbra. Being different actually works, has for centuries, and despite the rising divorce rates, escalating numbers of failed relationships, and the pandemic of insomnia caused by the devastating news that Paris Hilton broke up with yet another boyfriend, men and women, by and large, are still happier *with* each other than they are alone.

Whether we consider the dynamics of perceived male privilege or a newfound female sense of entitlement, it doesn't make either one of them right. What is needed is for the two sexes to bury the hatchet, search for ways to recognize and appreciate gender differences, and then exploit each other's strengths in ways that benefit both. Maybe it's time men and women *celebrate* their differences instead of going to war over them. Why do we have a battle of the sexes anyway? Why does either one need to be superior to the other? We don't need a battle between the sexes; we need a blooming of them. At the very least, it would cut down on the dry cleaning bills.

30

THE ULTIMATE SECRET

Women have insatiable appetites for secrets. In fact, secrets are to women what DVDs of wet T-shirt contests are to men; they simply cannot get enough of them. Yet, a funny thing happened on the way to completing this book. Countless women said they want one secret in particular, but not just any secret. They want the ultimate secret. They want to know the premier piece of inside information that resides incognito in the deepest, darkest confines of every man's head. They want Secret No. 31, and they want it now!

There is good news and bad news with this one. The good news is, I have such a secret. The bad news is that I would be violating the unwritten code among men if I spilled that one. The name of this book is *Secrets from Inside the Clubhouse*, not *All the Way Inside the Clubhouse*. It's kind of like a woman's purse. There's only so much of it a man is allowed to see.

But since I'm surrounded at the moment by a team of editors, all women, and all standing with hands on hips tapping their feet and focusing a stare that could burn a hole in my keyboard, I'd better fess up fast.

The one secret that will really take women deep inside the clubhouse, the one piece of classified, totally confidential, top secret information few men would ever reveal is actually a three-fold secret. It is also one that could even be life-altering in practice and unendingly powerful in effect. Secret No. 31, the ultimate secret that men think but don't say is, *"We want a woman to be our companion, not our competitor; our partner, not our parent; and our friend, not our foe."*

Men don't want to compete with their girlfriends or wives; they have to do enough of that everywhere else in everyday life with everybody else. They want their better halves to be the safe harbor they can take respite in when they need to escape the storm. More than anything else, they want true companions, someone to travel through life with them, side by side, not racing against them. Ed, the business man from Laguna Hills, California, we heard from earlier says he's waiting to find such a girl with whom he can share his life.

"I'm forty years old and I've never been married. I plan on getting married, and I don't plan on ever getting divorced. But until I meet just the right girl, I'm not willing to make a commitment. People say guys are afraid of commitment. Maybe some are, but I'm not. I'll make the commitment, but I want to make it only once. I just want a woman to share life with me as my ultimate companion, somebody I can share everything with. I don't want a woman I feel I'm constantly competing with. I have to do that with people at work every day. I want my home to be my sanctuary and the companionship of my wife to be my home."

Men also want women to share life with them as partners, not as parents. Remember our discussion of individuation? When a woman orders a man about, or critically repudiates him, he feels mothered and therefore less individuated. Trevor, the lawyer from Phoenix, Arizona, says his wife is his partner in more ways than one.

"I've been practicing law for twenty-three years, and my wife has been my partner through all of them. She helped support me when I was in law school and continues to support me not only as my partner in life but also as my partner in our law practice. People always ask me how we've been able to make that work, living and working together. It's easy; we're really partners. Neither one of us bosses the other around or tries to run the show, at the office or at home. We're fifty-fifty partners in all we do. We discussed it and decided long ago that's the only way we both would be happy with it."

Men grew up being controlled by their mothers. And though that's not a bad thing, after being on the receiving end of the necessary instructions and injunctions that came with childhood, they don't really fancy continuing to hear them from their girlfriends and wives. While parenting is unilateral by design, partnerships are bilateral by choice. Men want partners; they already have parents.

Finally, men want a woman to be a friend, not a foe. Doug, the salesman from Seattle, Washington, has had both and knows what he *doesn't* want now. "I'm not totally sure I know what I want in the ideal woman, but I can definitely tell you what I don't want. I don't want any woman who can't be my friend. In my experience, I've found that when it was all about lust and sex, it would only last so long, and the girl ended up being more of an enemy than a friend. We tried to force a relationship that really didn't exist. It made for some pretty ugly endings. I want a girl who will be a real friend to me, not someone who fights with me. Real friends have their spats, but then they get over them in favor of the friendship. To me, the ideal girlfriend or wife doesn't fight, she befriends. After that, the sex is a bonus."

Men know how to be friends with other men. They wish they knew how to do the same with women. If women only knew how much men appreciate their friendship, it might change their entire view of the male species. This is perhaps the area where women can be most helpful to men. Men just wish women would show them how to be good friends by *living* it, not by mandating it. Secret No. 31 is more than just the ultimate secret, it's the one women need more than any other. It could be called the secret way to catch and keep a man.

Men really do want a companion, a partner, and a friend. Women wise to Secret No. 31 know that competing with men, parenting them, and battling against them will likely drive them away. They also know that men were taught growing up they are supposed to bond with other men (companionship), to take charge of their own life and create another with a woman (partnership), and to separate from parental control and value participating with others (friendship). How ironic it is that so many men think women are better than them, or at least more sophisticated. If women really are the superior sex, this would be the ideal time to act like it.

For Guys Only

If you're a woman reading this book, you've just finished. Thanks for reading it, and please tell all of your friends about it so I can make enough money to buy a new pair of running shoes. I may need them sooner than I think. Please put the book down now and go have a Häagen-Dazs or one of those ten-dollar coffees at Starbucks. What follows is not for you. It's just for guys, specifically, guys inside the clubhouse. I've spent over two hundred pages sharing secrets men think but don't say. You don't need to know what is said in the last two and a half. This bit is just for men.

Okay, guys, now that we're alone together, I've got a few things I want to share with you, but whatever you do, don't tell any women about this. I may have given them thirty-one secrets, but the one I'm about to give you trumps them all! Remember, there's a code among men; don't violate it.

There could be a real advantage for us in conceding that women are the superior sex. We all know we don't want to be women. It's enough that we have to turn our heads and cough, bend over and take a finger up our butts, and worry about prostate cancer. Women have to spread their legs and slap them in the stirrups and *still* put up with the finger routine. Plus, they have to deal with walking in heels, shaving their legs, enduring that infamous monthly fun cycle, sitting on public toilets to pee, and yes, getting pregnant!

And there is so much pressure on women to look good. They're injecting Botox into their faces, collagen into their lips, and silicone into their boobs. They jack with hairspray, lip gloss, makeup, and hair coloring, too. Admit it, most of us would rather don the fatigues and fall into a foxhole somewhere! Staring down the barrel of an M-16 seems a whole lot easier.

We probably should cease the battle and agree that women *are* the superior sex. We're really just second-class citizens at best. Our behavior proves it. We scratch in public, spit in public, fart in public, and pick our noses in public. We don't listen well; leave toilet seats up, though we've been asked to put them down thousands of times; and typically don't know how to wear clothes that match. We may have the brawn, and even that's questionable these days, and we're better at reading maps, but honestly, if we swallow our pride and get real here, we've got to admit that women really are tougher than we are. How many of us would sign up *just one time* for a chance to put up with all of that stuff the ladies have to tolerate *every freakin' day*? And how many of us would jump at the chance to be pregnant?

Women are growing intellectually, emotionally, and professionally, while most of us, speaking in generalizations, remain static. It is often said that acceptance of a problem is the first step toward recovery, so let's be honest. We screw up all the time, and a whole lot more than they do. It must be true, just think about how rarely we correct them versus how often they're correcting us! The proportional differences are mind-boggling!

But there is good news for us. We can use this knowledge about women to our advantage. So here's my big secret for every one of you out there who's lucky enough to be reading this. It's really quite simple: Whenever we make a mistake, screw up, you know, blow it somehow and find ourselves in the doghouse, we can relax and not worry about it. Because after all is said and done, we're just guys being guys—you know, inferior human beings doing what inferior human beings (guys) do. So the secret? Just do it!

The women won't be at all surprised by our behavior. In fact, when you think about it, if we *didn't* screw up all the time, they wouldn't know what to do with us. It would upend their cognitive anticipatory schemata as to what constitutes normal behavior for men. They'd probably buy some lame self-help book with a weird title like *How to Be the Ideal Gatherer When Your Hunter Is at Home* just to be able to cope with us.

Women wouldn't know what to do with *quality* men who live right, work hard, and keep their mistakes to a minimum. They'd read the book from cover to cover while scrambling about searching for some reason to correct us, dictate some half-baked injunction, or issue a new list of official mandates. But what would they do about their perceived congenital predisposition to control not only the hearth and home, but the very swain who lives there? In other words, what would they do with us? If we actually became what they want us to become, it could really screw up a lot of women. Remediation would be a thing of the past. So if you think about it, we're actually doing them a favor, because we're doing a pretty good job of living down to their expectations.

But, here's the *best* part of all. Being typical guys all the time can actually be an advantage for us. Knowing we're going to screw up again and again, in a strange kind of way actually gives us permission to do it. It's expected, so each time we're guilty of some indiscretion or we misbehave in whatever way the superior being determines, we're okay. We may not be off the hook right away, and we may have to live with the consequences appropriate to the crime, but whatever the penance, we'll live to see another day, eat another meal, and watch another football game.

So relax, guys, because it's just like having a revolving get-out-of-jail-free card. Just put it on the tab, girls; we'll square up with you at the end of the month. And maybe if we're lucky, if we're *really* lucky, if the stars all align in perfect harmony, there's peace on earth, all is right with the world, and that tail wind of luck is at our backs, we might actually be sentenced to spend some time in solitary confinement! At least there, if we say something in the forest and a girl isn't there to hear it, we aren't necessarily wrong. But what do I know, I'm just a guy.

ABOUT THE AUTHOR

Ron Stout is a certified, perhaps certifiable, baby boomer. Over the course of three-plus decades, he has completed multiple tours of duty as a faithful conscript on the blood-stained terra firma of relationship battles. He is also a decorated veteran of two conjugal wars.

As a man, he has experienced the sweeping changes in gender roles since the sixties. As an academic, he has a BA in Psychology and an MS in Counseling and Human Development. He also teaches college courses in educational psychology, human development, and personal and social adjustment.

Ron lives somewhere over the clouds, under the rainbow, a stone's throw as the crow flies, just the other side of reality. He prefers to spend most of his time somewhere between the 30th and 35th parallel with anyone who bathes regularly and can speak in complete sentences.